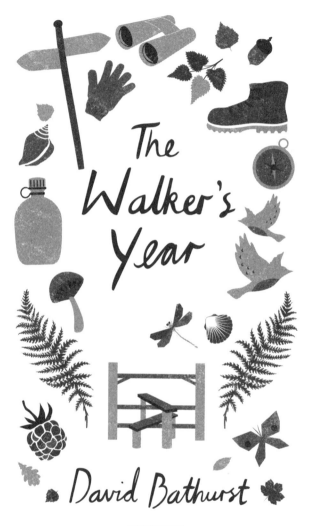

The Walker's Year

David Bathurst

summersdale

THE WALKER'S YEAR

Summersdale Publishers Ltd
46 West Street
Chichester
West Sussex
PO19 1RP
UK

www.summersdale.com

Printed and bound in the Czech Republic

ISBN: 978-1-84953-696-7

Substantial discounts on bulk quantities of Summersdale books are available to corporations, professional associations and other organisations. For details contact Nicky Douglas by telephone: +44 (0) 1243 756902, fax: +44 (0) 1243 786300 or email: nicky@summersdale.com.

A note from the author

I LOVE WALKING and have done throughout my adult life. The wonderful thing I have found about walking is that it is an all-year and all-weather pastime. Whatever the time of year and whatever the weather there is something to observe and enjoy. A spring walk offers crystal-clear days, hilltop views that go on for ever, and the joy of seeing the countryside burst into life; a summer's day brings sun-drenched walks through woodland to the sound of cricket and grasshopper; autumn promises the gold, russet and rich brown of turning leaves, and the bounty of berries from our trees and bushes; and winter has its own special magic of snow-capped conifers and mountains and restless seas throwing up columns of foam into the crisp air. Daylight is not even a pre-requisite to walking enjoyment: a walk in darkness, providing you're properly equipped and are visible, can produce unforgettable sightings of stars as well as night life such as hedgehogs and bats.

IT IS THIS great diversity of opportunity for the walker in Britain throughout the year that this book celebrates, providing a wealth of advice and recommendations for walkers for each month of the year, and whether you just fancy a short stroll or you yearn for some adventure on your walks, you'll find something here for you, winter or summer, autumn or spring. I hope you enjoy the journey as much as I have, and will continue to do.

January

Landscape

NEW YEAR'S DAY, and while it's likely to be still dark as you rise in the morning, and will be for many more days, there's a feeling of having turned the corner – and with it, the certain knowledge that from now till late June every day will bring a little more light than the previous one, and so more time for walking.

'JANUARY BRINGS THE snow, makes our feet and fingers glow' (Sara Coleridge). January is the most likely month for the walker to be able to tramp in the snow – but make the most of it as in Britain there are on average just 16.5 days per annum when snow is on the ground. The Scottish average is a more generous 27.7 days per annum.

EVEN IF THERE'S no lying snow, the walker must still wrap up warm and expect the year's coldest temperatures in January. All of the record cold temperatures for Britain occurred in this month (the lowest minimum temperature recorded was -27.2 degrees Celsius at Braemar, Scotland, on 10 January 1982 and the lowest maximum was –11.3 degrees Celsius at Newport, Shropshire the following day).

WALKERS IN BRITAIN have it easier than hikers in many other European countries. Very icy and snowy winters in Britain are relatively unusual due to the warming of the Atlantic by the so-called North Atlantic Drift, pushing milder, wetter air in from the west. Indeed on the island of Islay, off the west coast of Scotland, snowdrops may be seen carpeting the woodland floor by the end of the month.

DURING ONE OF the milder winters, prepare to be walking in the rain, especially in western Scotland – on average Kinlochewe, on the north-west coast of Scotland, receives 309.3 mm of rain every January, compared with 76.2 mm in Bognor Regis on the south coast and 83.4 mm in Sheffield, south Yorkshire.

WHILE SNOW IS a lot less likely further south, even in sunny Bognor Regis in West Sussex the average daytime maximum temperature in January is only 7.8 degrees Celsius. Bracing walking weather indeed, so layer up, have the waterproofs handy and keep moving.

DESPITE THE FACT that the days are getting longer, there's still not much light. In southern England there are just over 8 hours in January from sunrise to sunset, but this goes down to just under 7 hours in northern Scotland, the sun not rising till 8.45 a.m. GMT on 1 January and setting at just before 3.40 p.m. Something to remember when planning a January walk.

January

DURING THE LONG January nights in Scotland, if you can cope with the cold, the night sky yields its own treasure for the explorer on foot – the Northern Lights or aurora borealis. Though this isn't exclusively a January phenomenon, this month is generally regarded as the best time to spot these playful streaks of colour caused by wind from the sun colliding with magnetic particles in the Earth's atmosphere. Scotland provides the best views of this phenomenon, from skies untarnished by light pollution.

JANUARY ON THE Cotswold Way brings 50 shades of grey: the brooding grey of the winter sky against the lighter grey of the farmsteads and dry stone walls, pockets of weeks-old snow glued to hilltops unwilling to accept a welcome thaw, freezing mud attending each field corner, footpaths deserted by the fair-weather hikers, visitor attractions in hibernation, darkness hardly able to wait to claim the final vestiges of the day, the urgent rush of footsteps on fierce concrete to catch the last bus.

A JANUARY MORNING on the cliffs of north Somerset offers acres of heather stripped of its August glory, huddling beneath a twin carpeting of frost and snow. The heather-covered hilltops are not places to linger on but to conquer – a frightening silence in the woods around little Culbone church, the snow-capped trees still, pockets of watery blue in an otherwise white sky, the sanctuary of Lynmouth still many miles off.

MUD MAY BE glorious to the hippopotamus but in
January it can be especially hazardous to walkers,
either because of its volume – caused by excessive
rainfall – or because it's concealed by layers of ice.
The risk of getting lost, obstructed or cut off may
be averted by keeping to bridleways, public byways
or metalled roads in the worst weather. Bridleways
and byways will be open to cyclists and horse riders
as well as walkers and, by definition, will be wider,
better defined and better surfaced. Note that a PUBLIC
byway is open to all traffic but a RESTRICTED byway
is not open to mechanically propelled vehicles.

OAKS, LIKE ALL deciduous trees, will be devoid
of leaves or colour in January, but their imposing
bark and spreading branches create their very own
architectural patterns. When walking in a forest of
deciduous trees watch especially for the oaks, beneath
the bark of which millions of insects will be feeding.

A JANUARY MORNING on Thorney Island brings the
walker acres and acres of flat reclaimed grassland
waving morosely in the rain-bearing south-westerly
breeze. Wild geese congregate on Pilsey Island and then
sweep into the vast acres of sky in tightly-disciplined
formation, the sand spit of East Head visible across
Chichester Harbour, emptied of its summer crowds.

WHILE JANUARY SEES few flowering plants, watch on
your January walks for the widespread yellow flowers
of the winter aconite, the pea-green flowers of the
stinking hellebore in southern woodland,
the yellow flowers of the spurge laurel
in woodlands in England and Wales,
and for early flowering snowdrops in
gardens, woods and hedges.

Wildlife

IT FOLLOWS THAT snow is more likely to be lying in Scotland and those brave enough to walk in the Scottish Highlands in the depths of winter may observe the remarkable phenomenon of ptarmigans, stoats and mountain hares that have been turning white in order to blend in with their surroundings for both defensive and predatory purposes.

IN THE CAIRNGORMS in north-east Scotland, brave January walkers may be rewarded with the sight of reindeer and golden eagles. With eyesight ten times more powerful than that of a human, the golden eagle will hunt aggressively for whatever food the unyielding landscape can offer including ptarmigan, mountain hare or grouse.

THE LOW TEMPERATURES in January provide real challenges for our non-migratory birds. As you walk in January, watch for tits and finches foraging in the countryside, flocking together for safety in their quest for nourishment. Woodland may bring sightings of the great, blue and coal tit. In gardens and hedgerows, watch for sparrows foraging for grain and seeds, while look to ploughed fields for red kites in search of earthworms.

ANIMALS MUST WORK hard to survive too during this month. Look out for deer feeding from low-hanging leaves on evergreen trees, and groups of short-eared owls hunting over rough grassland in southern Britain. Crisp cold windless winter days provide ideal conditions for barn owls to hunt. Meanwhile, foxes probe the snow for meals of creatures that haven't survived the harsh conditions.

A COASTAL WALK in January may provide sightings of large numbers of overwintering birds which survive by feeding at low tide and gather in huge flocks to sit out the change of tide. In particular, mudflats off the south coast provide particularly good opportunities for birdwatching walkers in January to view curlews, grey plovers, oystercatchers, lapwings, redshanks, avocets and dunlins.

SOME JANUARYS LATTERLY have been exceedingly mild, temperatures climbing towards the mid-teens Celsius. This may bring an unexpected crop of wildlife into the countryside including some species of butterfly such as comma, brimstone or red admiral; some birds may be confused into nesting early, leaves may start to unfurl and flowering daffodils and primroses aren't unknown.

A MILD JANUARY is good news for the walker perhaps. But a cold snap may be disastrous for these early starters. In particular a frost may kill early-flowering plants and hibernating creatures awaking early may not find enough food to subsist. So enjoy the unscheduled arrivals while they're there for sadly they may not make it to 'proper' spring.

Where to Walk in January

JANUARY IS THE ideal month for you to get to know your own locality on foot, given the shortage of daylight and the less than predictable weather. Not only will regular exercise keep you in trim and serve as good training for endeavours later in the year, but it will enable you to find out much more about your own area.

JANUARY IS A great month for venturing out into the flat lowland countryside where you can gaze up at skies that seem to stretch for ever and then train the binoculars on wintering birds that frequent our wetlands, estuaries, lakes, flooded meadows and harbours. Leave the mountains for longer and sunnier days!

PAGHAM HARBOUR, WEST SUSSEX, provides some wonderfully scenic and unspoilt walking and offers sights of blacktailed godwit, brent geese, little egret, little tern, lapwing, dunlin and pintail among many others. Further west, Slimbridge, by the Severn in Gloucestershire, offers 120 acres supporting a huge number of ducks, swans including Bewick's swans, peregrines, merlins and geese including the rare Hawaiian geese.

HEADING NORTH AND east, Martin Mere in Ormskirk, Lancashire is a wetland nature reserve with habitats for birds from across the world. A huge number of birds may be on display in January including pink-footed geese, wigeon, whooper swan, snow goose and hen harrier. And the similarly-named Minsmere, near Saxmundham, Suffolk, is an RSPB nature reserve with a high diversity of bird species particularly ducks, swans and geese.

NORTH OF THE border, Caerlaverock Wetland Centre, Dumfries in southern Scotland, is described as a 'winter feast' with species including barnacle geese, knot, pintail, oystercatcher, white teal, goldeneye, dunlin, grey plover and golden plover.

TRY WALKING A section or sections of a lesser-known named path in your locality. They're identified on the back covers of all Ordnance Survey Explorer maps, and you'll find there's one near you. They will be well signed and clearly delineated on the Explorer maps themselves; they vary greatly in length, but all are manageable either in stages or all at once, and will provide a real sense of achievement when completed.

WHY NOT TAKE up a new hobby for a new year and try geocaching? This is hi-tech treasure hunting on foot, using GPS navigation devices to locate boxes containing 'treasure' left by other walkers. Google 'geocaching' to get started and you'll find there's 'treasure' to be had within walking distance of your front door. It's also great training in navigational skills for walkers.

January Wisdom

THE DARK DAYS of January can feel very flat after the excitement of Christmas. So cheer yourself up during the month by planning some walking objectives for the year – perhaps using some of the ideas highlighted later in this book.

SCENICALLY, THERE ARE few sights more awe-inspiring in Britain than snow-covered mountains in winter. If you're determined to climb one in January, you must be properly prepared, clothed and shod. Boots alone won't do; you'll need crampons, spiked attachments for your boots that will give them a grip on snow and ice. Get specialist help – NOT just online advice.

WITH EXTREMES OF all kinds of bad weather most common in January, wherever you're walking, never put yourself in danger from exposure or hypothermia or other effects of snow, ice, rain and wind. In wet weather you need a good quality waterproof jacket. The jacket must be breathable, that is, able to let air in and sweat out, being made of material that picks up moisture and carries it away from the body. It should ideally be lightweight; if you're concerned about cold, add some layers underneath.

DO REMEMBER THAT on many surfaces, especially in dry conditions, trainers or stout shoes may be perfectly adequate and more comfortable than boots. Experience will tell you what works best – but it's always best to err on the side of caution.

January

IN COLD WEATHER, several thin layers of clothing are better than one or two very thick ones, giving you flexibility all the time you're out. Don't forget gloves and a hat capable of covering the ears. Don't worry about a visit from the fashion police – your comfort and safety comes first. Make sure you take hot drinks and high-energy foods with you if walking a long distance in the cold.

BOOTS ARE THE most important things to get right. When fitting boots there should be enough room to poke a forefinger behind the heel, and the toes should just touch the boot at the front. Remember to allow for the feet to swell when they get too hot. Undertake modest local walks in your new boots so you can 'break them in', that is, make them conform to the shape of your feet and maximise comfort. It's a bad idea to walk long distances in them straight away, though.

STOCK UP ON socks as well; it's a good plan to wear two pairs of socks while walking, as these produce a cushioned effect and will absorb a great deal of moisture. Opt for loop stitch, a special form of knitting which looks like towelling and covers the seams, thus making blisters much less likely.

COLD IS NOT only demoralising, it is also potentially dangerous and the need for warmth becomes all-consuming. Under normal conditions the pores of the skin excrete water vapour but when the body is cold the pores close and in an attempt to increase warmth by stimulation the body will start to shiver. Shivering should be avoided where possible because the body will waste valuable energy in an attempt to regulate its temperature.

Notes

1
....

2
....

3
....

4
....

5
....

6
....

7
....

8
....

9
....

10
....

11
....

12
....

13
....

14
....

January

15
....

16
....

17
....

18
....

19
....

20
....

21
....

22
....

23
....

24
....

25
....

26
....

27
....

28
....

29
....

30
....

31
....

February

Landscape

CANDLEMAS DAY FALLS on 2 February, on which the snowdrop is traditionally expected to begin flowering. Its appearance is regarded as an indication that winter is on the wane. Like crocuses, snowdrops remain in the ground as perennial bulbs so they can store energy during the winter period and then appear as the temperatures rise. So diarise a snowdrop walk as soon after 2 February as the weather allows.

OTHER FLOWERS MAY make their first appearance in February, especially in the mild south-west. These include the primrose and also the celandine, whose custard-yellow flowers open when the sun shines and close when the sun disappears. When walking in February look out also for catkins hanging from the branches of hazel trees.

A WOODLAND WALK in February may be rewarded by the appearance in flower, again if mild weather allows, of common gorse, sweet violet in England and Wales, and mezereon in central and southern England. Watch in gardens for the appearance of the delicate blue dwarf iris.

WALKERS SHOULD BE on their guard, as snow remains a notional possibility in February: indeed some weather experts predict that global warming could disrupt the Gulf Stream and plunge Great Britain into much colder winters. Not good news for walkers!

HOWEVER IT IS winds that have provided the main weather headlines in February in recent times. High winds can be more dangerous for walkers than rain and snow with the risk of walkers being blown over by the wind especially in exposed areas. Be prepared to postpone your planned walk rather than take the risk.

GENERALLY OUR WEATHER is colder and windier the further north in Britain you go, and it is a fact that extreme weather is much less likely to make headline news if it happens in northern Britain than in the so-called 'soft south' – remember that when planning a walking holiday in winter in northern England and Scotland.

FOR COASTAL WALKERS in February, the most menacing wind is that which blows from off the land. John Merrill, when undertaking his walk round the entire coast of Great Britain in 1978, recalls how on 18 February he was walking from Port Isaac to Boscastle on the north Cornwall coast. He remembers that he could not stand upright and the only way to safeguard himself from being blown over the cliff edge was to cling to a barbed wire fence.

THERE ARE SIGNIFICANT variations in rainfall across Britain in February. The Sussex coast averages just 49.6 mm of rain and nine rain days during this month, Sheffield 60.4 mm and 10.5 rain days but those walking on the west coast of Scotland in February will be more likely to get wet than stay dry; it amasses 238 mm of rain and an average of 18.3 wet days out of February's 28/29 days.

ANYONE VISITING THE Lake District, which attracts more rain than most places in England, can expect some rain in February. Alan Plowright recalls his February trip to the Lakes, and the Lake District rain which he discovered 'cascades vertically downwards, pounds itself into the ground and rebounds ferociously to a height of several feet.'

SCOTLAND MAY NOT always be wetter but it is darker – important for the walker to bear in mind. At the beginning of February, sunrise is a good 30 minutes later in northern Scotland than in southern England and sunset comes just under 20 minutes earlier.

I REMEMBER THE hilltop known as the Trundle above Chichester in West Sussex one early February lunchtime: the blue morning sky submitting inexorably to a covering of thick dark cloud and the total obliteration of the Isle of Wight and then Chichester Cathedral itself by the approaching deluge; a vicious wind pummelling the outer ring, the first few tentative drops and then an explosion from the skies, fiery arrows of hail stinging the cheeks in the rush for shelter.

WALKERS IN FEBRUARY need to be prepared for anything and there can be wonderful surprises: John Merrill recalls a great moment in his walk along the north Cornwall and Devon coast in February, following some hefty blizzards and low cloud. 'I watched a beautiful sunset explode across the horizon and saw the fiery ball lower into the sea.'

EVERGREENS SUCH AS Scots pine, juniper and yew continue to thrive on the coldest February days. They have evolved to withstand the worst of the winter weather, their sap containing resin that stops ice crystals from forming.

I REMEMBER THE Downs Link, a railway footpath in Surrey between Cranleigh and Shalford one Monday February afternoon: early rain ceasing to leave a still, sterile landscape, the January snows delaying the arrival of spring colour, the grass a listless damp greeny-grey, drops of water clinging to the branches of the still naked silver birches, the unwary boot slithering on the patches of mud beneath the feet.

MANY OF OUR streams and rivers are so-called winterbournes – they appear only when the water levels in the chalk aquifers are sufficiently high, and with the most sustained rainfall coming in winter, they will be likely to be at their most active in February, providing potential for delightful waterside walks. Similarly, our great waterfalls such as High Force near Middleton-in-Teesdale and Hardraw Force near Hawes, both on the Pennine Way, will be at their most powerful in winter after sustained rainfall.

Wildlife

IN THE PINE forests of the Scottish Highlands, the Scottish crossbills may have chicks in their nests as early as February, and intrepid February walkers may observe many other species of birds nesting and breeding this month, including rooks, ravens and grey herons.

IF YOUR FEBRUARY rambling includes a walk by a pond, watch for the frogspawn, tough clusters of jelly which may appear in ponds during this month. It can in theory appear at any time from New Year onwards in mild winters. It's so tough that even if the surface of the water freezes over, it may still survive underneath.

MANY BIRDS WINTERING in Great Britain will still be here in February, so if the January weather was too inclement, it's worth venturing to lakes, gravel pits and reservoirs this month to see large flocks of wigeon, teal, shoveler, goosander, goldeneye and smew.

ONE OF THE most spectacular sights a winter walker may see, February being as good a time as any, is that of a flock of thousands of wading birds fleeing the predatory peregrine falcon, the signal given being a sharp alarm call from the first bird to see the threat.

February

As you walk in the February countryside you may be pleasantly surprised to hear a large amount of birdsong. What you may be hearing is males singing to repel rival males and win mates for themselves. Typical early bird singers in February will be song thrushes, mistle thrushes and robins. The lack of foliage in deciduous trees makes it easier to see and identify birds among the branches.

During this month, walkers may experience magpies gathering in large flocks, something they do towards the end of winter. Remember 'five for silver, six for gold, seven is for a secret never to be told!'

If you're hoping for dry weather in February, remember this proverb: 'If in February there be no rain, 'tis neither good for hay nor grain.' There is considerable truth in this, as February rain will be more easily absorbed into the soil and keep the chalk aquifers filled ahead of the drier summer months. So if you're out walking in February, don't curse the rain too much!

Where to Walk in February

THE DAYS ARE getting a little longer but the weather can often remain very unsettled in February. With that in mind, this is the ideal month to do a home-based historic themed walk, so if the weather deteriorates you're not far from base and can curtail your walk if need be. Look on your map for a historical feature e.g. an old church, castle ruin, fortification that you've not previously visited, and walk there.

COMBINE A HISTORIC quest with some scenic walking by visiting the Norfolk Broads. Stay at Horning or Wroxham, enjoy the off-season tranquillity of the waters, and visit some of the many windmills, those at How Hill and Horsey being particularly impressive.

GET IN TOUCH with our transport history and try a disused railway walk. Many disused railways have been turned into excellent footpaths. Walk part or all of the Downs Link between Shoreham-by-Sea in West Sussex and Shalford in Surrey, virtually all of its 35 miles are along the course of two old railway lines, with many memorabilia from the old lines still in situ including platforms, bridges and level crossing gates.

ANOTHER SPLENDID DISUSED railway walk is the Camel Trail in Cornwall, running for 18 miles from Wenford Bridge to Padstow via Bodmin and Wadebridge through the wooded countryside of Upper Camel Valley and then the Camel Estuary. The trail runs through a Site of Special Scientific Interest (SSSI) and nature conservation area.

A SHORTER BUT equally charming rail trail is the Brampton Valley Way which runs for 14 miles between Boughton Crossing, Northampton, to Little Bowden Crossing, Market Harborough, highlights including Brixworth Country Park and Pitsford Water.

GIVEN THE UNPREDICTABILITY of British weather in February, try one of the easier long-distance routes such as the Ridgeway National Trail which runs for 85.5 miles from Overton in Wiltshire to Ivinghoe in Buckinghamshire – arguably the ultimate journey back in time. Its western half, through Wiltshire and Berkshire, passes several prehistoric sites of huge interest including Avebury, Barbury Castle, Wayland Smithy and Uffington White Horse. It's never far from civilisation if the weather changes unexpectedly for the worse.

FEBRUARY'S OFTEN STORMY weather brings impressive seas. Providing you stay safe, there is real exhilaration in watching waves crash against the shoreline, whether you do this from a sandy or shingle beach (perhaps combing the shingle to see what the tide has washed in, including sea creatures and sea shells), a harbour wall at a small seaside town or village such as Lyme Regis in Dorset or Mousehole in Cornwall, or the pier of a large seaside city or town. But NEVER put yourself at risk. Stay well back from the sea and be prepared to retreat further as necessary.

February Wisdom

HAVING DECIDED DURING the long January nights where you'd like to walk this year, plan and book it now. Remember that a train journey booked online three months ahead may cost considerably less than half what it will cost if booked at the last minute. Take care when booking places to stay; before confirming anything, check how far your proposed accommodation is from your planned walking – will you want to walk an extra mile or three at the end of a long day?

IF BOOKING IN connection with a walk on a long-distance path, check whether there's a baggage carrying service available. Walking unencumbered by a heavy pack may make all the difference, especially if you're new to long-haul walking.

IF YOU'RE ON a strict budget but want to 'go places' this year, consider joining the Youth Hostels Association. Youth Hostels aren't the formidable establishments they once were, there's no upper age limit despite their name, and they offer overnight accommodation at very reasonable prices. They're also a great way to make friends with other walkers.

ANOTHER ORGANISATION WORTH joining at this time of year is the Ramblers. They'll put you instantly in touch with fellow walking enthusiasts and experts and offer you myriad opportunities for guided walks should you be unwilling to venture out on your own.

IF YOUR THEME-BASED walking takes you across fields, you may well encounter cattle. Cows are normally quite harmless but very inquisitive. Don't be alarmed if they all turn in your direction and/or head towards you, and in particular don't panic if a herd of bullocks or heifers gallops in your direction; they will skid to a halt a safe distance away.

ADULT BULLS ARE another matter. While bulls should not be running freely in fields crossed by public paths, it does still happen. If you see a bull in the field you're in, get out fast, if possible without attracting the animal's attention. The bull is a clumsy creature and you should be able to dodge it if it comes towards you – but keep calm.

IF YOU DECIDE to visit the coast this month to watch the crash of the waves on a stormy day, stay safe. A single wave could wash you out to sea if you were caught in its path. The same applies if you venture to one of our waterfalls when in full spate – enjoy it from the safety of adjoining pathways and be content with that.

Notes

1
....

2
....

3
....

4
....

5
....

6
....

7
....

8
....

9
....

10
....

11
....

12
....

13
....

14
....

February

15
....

16
....

17
....

18
....

19
....

20
....

21
....

22
....

23
....

24
....

25
....

26
....

27
....

28
....

29
....

March

Landscape

ALTHOUGH AT THE beginning of March it's dark for longer than it's light, 21 March sees the vernal equinox when days and nights are of the same length – great news for walkers. And it gets better. It used to be thought that around the equinox there was a greater risk of high winds, known as equinoctial gales, but scientific research suggests that this is a myth, and it's no more likely than at any other time of year that we will see such gales.

BETTER STILL, THE last weekend of March sees the clocks going forward an hour. That's one hour less sleep but by the end of the month sunset in southern England isn't till 7.36 p.m. and in Scotland it's nearer 8 p.m. So start enjoying evening walks after work, and perhaps leave the car in the garage and incorporate some walking into your commute.

TEMPERATURES ARE CREEPING up. The average daytime maximum temperature right across the country has risen from around 7 to around 10 degrees Celsius, and rainfall in parts of England is considerably less in March than in January – in Sheffield, for instance, average rainfall reduces from 83 mm in January to 63 mm in March.

March

MARCH SEES THE flowering of the wonderfully named butterbur, notable for its enormous heart-shaped leaves, which measure up to one metre across, and thick spikes of pinkish flower heads. It is widespread in most of Great Britain on damp ground.

SNOW IS BY no means uncommon in March despite this month seeing the start of spring. March 12 2013 brought a covering of snow to large parts of England leading to the closure of schools, and Easter 1975 was nicknamed a 'white Easter' with extensive snowfalls across the country and widespread lying snow. None of which helps planning your spring and Easter walking break!

ADVANTAGE MAY BE taken of a burst of warmth in mid- to late March to mow verges, lawns and greens for the first time of the year, so walkers in parks and gardens may enjoy that most delicious aroma of freshly cut grass, synonymous with soft warm days.

I RECALL LATE March in Essex: Essex, not normally associated with mountainous scenery, but here on Chrishall Common, its highest ground, an intriguing and intricate collage of sudden dips and inclines, rain-washed green fields stretching many many miles, and pockets of stumpy wind-caressed woodland under a blanket of monochrome cloud.

I REMEMBER THE Pembrokeshire Coast Path on an unseasonably warm March Monday: morning mist lingering on the harbour and mineworkings of Porthgain, the stunning valley of Pwll Caerog and the maze of rocks of St David's Head, then a tentative hazy sun providing tantalisingly limited views across the sound to Ramsey Island, and then blazing afternoon sunlight giving an unforgettable picture of the natural arch below Porthllisky and the impossibly narrow harbour of Porthclais.

IN SOUTHERN PARTS of England, the daffodil may have appeared in February but is most closely associated with March. It's also known as the 'Lent lily' because the season of Lent, running from Ash Wednesday to Easter, always falls partially in March, whenever Easter is. A walk through a daffodil woodland provides a colourful, if bracing, experience – not least in March 2013 when despite spring having officially begun three days before, a walk among daffodils in a Sussex woodland needed thick jackets and even thicker gloves.

DAFFODILS AREN'T THE only splash of colour you'll see on your walks in March. Also in (yellow) flower this month will be the ubiquitous dandelion and common whitlow grass. In both woodland and grassland you may see the bluish flowers of the common dog violet and in damp peaty soil and marshes you may find the pinkish-white flowers of the bogbean.

March

Two types of saxifrage should be in flower in March; intrepid walkers on mountains in northern England, Wales and Scotland may see the small purple flowers of the purple saxifrage on mountain ledges and rocks, while shady stream banks in the north and west of Britain may offer up the yellow flowers of the golden saxifrage.

It's exciting to walk in March and see signs of spring. Look out in particular for sticky buds that appear on the branches of deciduous trees, buds that will, in a few weeks, have exploded into green life. But remember a hard winter and cold March may delay this process till April.

Sand drains superbly so even if the winter's been wet, a walk on sandy heathland in Dorset, Hampshire or Surrey is a great choice on a mild sunny March day.

Wildlife

THERE MAY BE just enough warmth in the March air to allow an early queen bumble bee to emerge and search for nectar. Queens may be seen as early as January and February but mid-March is more normal. They will cruise round early blooming flowers such as crocuses or primroses before alighting on them to feed on their nectar. To get into breeding condition a queen needs to visit more than 5,000 flowers every day.

IF YOU'RE VERY fortunate when field walking in March you may at this time of year see brown hares 'boxing' in which the female boxes the male in order to test his mettle. The two hares will box for only a few seconds then one will turn and scarper. Hence the expression 'mad as a March hare'.

As YOU WALK in the heathlands of Dorset, Hampshire or Surrey you may see adders that have emerged from their hiding places to bask in the sunshine to up their body temperature. Sandy soil is their preferred habitat. Adders only pose a threat if they themselves feel threatened so approach them with care.

BIRDWATCHING WALKERS NOTE, virtually all the resident songbirds such as thrushes, robins, wrens, dunnocks, greenfinches, chaffinches and tits are now singing, only stopping from time to time in order to find food – so they can gain the energy to continue to sing.

THE CHORUS IS joined by the first returning migrants from warmer climes. These may include the sand martin, wheatear (whose name derives from a phrase meaning 'white arse'!), little ringed plover and garganey – the only species of duck that comes to spend summer in Britain.

A REAL TREAT for observant walkers will be the sight of the great spotted woodpecker, with splendid black, white and crimson plumage, drumming against the bark of trees, an action designed, at what is the start of a breeding season, to repel rival males and attract a mate.

IT'S NOT ONLY among birds that breeding is now taking place. As you walk beside ponds, note that not just frogs but newts will have laid or be laying their spawn, while voles and mice are already raising what will be the first of many litters, and as foxes and badgers give birth, cubs will emerge from the earth or sett.

AT THE SAME time that migrant birds are returning to our shores, the birdwatching walker will notice how ducks, geese and swans that have spent the winter months on our estuaries, marshes and reservoirs will now be heading north to breed in the High Arctic, to return to us in winter. Joining them on their journey north will be waders such as the sanderling, turnstone and knot.

Where to Walk in March

FOR WALKERS WITH a love of great views, a sunny early spring day can provide greater clarity than the sunshine of high summer, when in any case thick hedges and trees in leaf can shorten the views. Check out the Internet and find the highest point in your county or local area. Many of them are very easily reached and provide tremendous views on a clear day.

AMONG THE BEST – and easiest – 'county highs' are Dunstable Down in Bedfordshire, Shining Tor in Cheshire, Bardon Hill in Leicestershire, Ebrington Hill in Warwickshire, Silverhill Wood in Nottinghamshire and Leith Hill in Surrey (though the latter is some distance from the nearest public transport).

FOR A RANGE of dramatic escarpment views, walk part or all of the 100-mile Cotswold Way from Bath in Somerset to Chipping Campden in Gloucestershire. Experience the huge panoramas from Stinchcombe Hill, Cleeve Hill and Broadway Tower, and the superb climax across Dover's Hill with lovely views across the Cotswolds and beyond.

THE MALVERNS IN Worcestershire are perhaps the ultimate in great gain, not much pain. Climbing majestically from the rolling but comparatively low-lying surrounding countryside, the summits, particularly Worcestershire Beacon and Herefordshire Beacon are easy to access from the nearby town of Great Malvern and have fine views to both Wales and the Midlands.

March

THE 67-MILE ISLE of Wight coastal path offers
tremendous views across the island itself but also over
the Solent to the mainland. Beat the Easter holiday
crowds and walk it in a long weekend, enjoying such
majestic viewpoints as Headon Hill, Tennyson Down
and the Yarborough Monument.

IN SOUTHERN COUNTIES, daffodils will be at their best
in March. For a particularly stunning wild daffodil
display, visit Lesnes Abbey Woods in the Greenwich
district of London, but any park or garden near you is
likely to be rich with them.

WALK ALONG THE shingle at Dungeness in Kent,
a marvellously atmospheric and remote spot, and
a bird watchers' paradise. During March it is a
popular landing ground for early
migrant birds. If the walking seems
arduous don't be surprised; the shingle
spit is 4 miles deep!

March Wisdom

By now you should have got plenty of use out of your new boots. Now you'll need to dubbin them – dubbin is a special kind of grease which if applied to the uppers, preserves their impermeability and makes them much more resistant to the many different types of terrain on which you may be using them. Avoid smearing dubbin on hard rubber soles. Follow the instructions on the packaging carefully and seek expert advice if necessary.

You may need to give some of your new walking clothing a good wash after your initial outings in it. Weatherproof garments should be cleaned only with warm water, gently soaking off any mud. Always hand wash, rather than machine wash, woollen sweaters, shirts and socks.

To stick or not to stick? A stick or walking pole may be invaluable in the wet or muddy conditions in which you may still be walking during March, in order to test the depth of mud or help you over boggy patches. It's been suggested it may also be useful for fending off inquisitive cattle. Walking poles can offer support and stability on even ground and reduce impact on knee and hip joints, good news for more mature walkers.

BE CAREFUL NOT to wield a pole or stick too freely, don't take one with you if lightning is about, and NEVER use it offensively against people or animals or you may be committing a criminal offence. A stick could also be dangerous if it got lodged amongst rocks because it could upset your balance and cause you to fall.

IF YOU DECIDE to climb a hilltop, don't forget your binoculars. These enable you to identify specific features and get a close-up on them which the naked eye cannot achieve. Binoculars range tremendously in price and quality and it's worth paying a little extra to make your hilltop experience that much more memorable.

ON A DAY or weekend trip you may be tempted to force the pace in your eagerness to reach your objective. Never rush in the countryside. There's always something to see which you will miss by being over hasty. Rushing may lead to sweating which affects your energy levels, and sometimes causes dehydration, one of the worst conditions a walker can have.

IN PARTICULAR RESIST the temptation to race up the first hill of the day and down the other side. In fact, start your walk at a rather slower pace than your normal speed, and ease yourself into your normal pace. You'll soon leave the quick starter far behind.

Notes

1
....

2
....

3
....

4
....

5
....

6
....

7
....

8
....

9
....

10
....

11
....

12
....

13
....

14
....

March

15
....

16
....

17
....

18
....

19
....

20
....

21
....

22
....

23
....

24
....

25
....

26
....

27
....

28
....

29
....

30
....

31
....

April

Landscape

'THERE WERE STARTLING yellow clouds of forsythia, trails of purple aubrietia; a young willow shook in a fountain of silver.' (Rachel Joyce).

DURING APRIL THERE will be over 13 hours of daylight wherever you are across Britain, and the days get much longer very quickly, with nearly 2 hours more daylight in the south at the end of the month than at the beginning, and just under two and a half hours more daylight in the far north – a lot of extra walking time.

I REMEMBER THE old railway line from Paddock Wood to Hawkhurst on a Saturday in late April: the first fresh dark green leaves bursting onto the horse chestnut trees, the long straight track lined with bluebells, the air thick with the aroma of wild garlic, more than a hint of potency in the warmth of the spring sunshine and the promise of languid summer days.

JOHN HILLABY RECALLS a gathering April storm in Cornwall soon after starting his end-to-end walk across Britain, and the sky turning from 'sickly yellow to apple green' while out to sea 'a line of billowy white clouds began to roll in like a mountain wave.'

April

'THE DAY WE walked through Dovedale was
fantastically cold for April and periods of sunshine
alternated with snowstorms – producing the most
glorious scenic effects which were not always
appreciated because of the ankle-deep mud. On the
return journey we climbed up the bank and sat on
a fallen tree to enjoy a picnic in the sunshine. Two
minutes later the food was bundled back in the
rucksack as a blizzard enveloped us.' (Mary Bathurst).

WEATHERWISE, APRIL MAY be unpredictable but
doesn't suffer the extremes of hot and cold that some
other months do, and better news still for walkers is
that southern parts on average enjoy twice as much
sunshine in April as in February. But the frost hasn't
quite gone: some parts of western Scotland will have
five frosts on average during this month.

APRIL IS FAMED for its showers and although on
a day of frequent downpours it's annoying for the
walker to have to keep reaching for the cagoule or
brolly, compensations come in the form
of rainbows, when sun and rain combine,
and often spectacular cloud formations,
no more so than that of the anvil-shaped
thundercloud, the cumulonimbus.

APRIL IS A wonderful month for woodland walking. Not only are leaves beginning to appear on deciduous trees but thousands of bluebells are blooming en masse in woods and forests; they are widespread throughout Britain, albeit appearing later the further north you go, and absent only from island groups to the north and west.

OUR DAMP MILD climate supports more than half the total world population of bluebells. They are able to store energy during autumn and winter in order to produce the spring flowers, each bulb producing up to six long green leaves. The flowering bluebells are particularly welcomed by early insects including their main pollinator, the bumble bee.

BESIDES THE BLUEBELL in April woodlands, you may also see the pale blue flowers of the bugle, the white and lilac flowers of the wood sorrel, the white and fragrant garlic mustard and ramson, the small white flowers of the pignut, and the pink flowers of herb Robert; and, in southern areas, bright blue forget-me-nots, small green flowers of the moschatel and the bright greenish-yellow flowers of the wood spurge.

TWO OTHER JOYS which appear in April are blossoms and tulips: the white blossoms of the blackthorn and wild cherry, and the diverse colours of flowering tulips including red, yellow and white – although these tend to be found in formal gardens rather than in the wild.

April

IF YOU PREFER an April walk in the open grassland or meadows, look for the small blue flowers of the thyme-leaved speedwell, the violet flowers of the wild pansy, the white flowers of the wild strawberry, the pale lilac of the cuckoo flower, and the pale lilac of the cornsalad.

IN UPLAND MOORS and in the mountains of northern Britain, April sees the appearance of the tiny pink six-petalled flowers of the crowberry, while if you decide to do some coastal walking, you may see steep cliffs carpeted with the pink flowers of the thrift, borne in globular heads on long stalks. Another common coastal plant which flowers now is the common scurvy grass with its white four-petalled flowers.

THE MARSH MARIGOLD flowers in April and you can enjoy quite dazzling displays of these bright yellow blooms in the Orkneys off north-east Scotland, but it's also possible to see these flowers throughout Britain, including in damp woodlands, marshes and pond margins.

Wildlife

FOR THE BIRDWATCHING walker, April is the peak time for the arrival of the bulk of migrant songbirds. In just a few weeks well over ten million individuals of more than 20 different species arrive, including warblers, flycatchers, chats, swallows, martins and swifts. If you happen to be in Berkeley Square, late April is the best time of the year to hear the song of another migrant bird, the nightingale.

MOST MIGRATING SONGBIRDS travel by night and once dawn approaches night travellers will look for suitable places to nest and feed, especially in bad weather. Southern headlands such as Portland Bill and Dungeness, or offshore islands off the south coast will see a huge concentration of migrant birds. They will then settle in different habitats, for instance the reed and sedge warbler to wetlands, the willow warbler and chiffchaff to the hedgerows, and wood warbler, pied flycatcher and redstart to the woodlands.

THE MOST DISTINCTIVE migrant birdsong of all will be heard from mid-April – that of the cuckoo, generally found in woodlands, scrub, moors, heaths and reedbeds. It is the male of the species, with slate grey upper parts and yellow legs and feet, that makes the 'coo… coo' call that all walkers will recognise: the female makes what are described as 'bubbling' calls.

April

NOT ONLY IS the cuckoo as a species famous for its extraordinary call, which persists into May, but for the fact that it doesn't make a nest itself but instead lays eggs in the nests of other birds. The eggs are laid singly in the nests of dunnock, reed warbler and meadow pipit.

APRIL SEES A number of butterflies appear: the first butterfly to emerge from a chrysalis is usually the orange tip, so named because of the two bright orange patches on the tips of the dark-tipped forewings of the male. Others seen in April include dingy and grizzled skippers, cabbage whites and pearl-bordered fritillaries.

AS YOU WALK in northern Britain, watch for another set of new arrivals. Although the lambing season varies across the country, it is in April that lambing is likely to start in the sheep-rich Yorkshire Dales and Lake District.

AND BY APRIL, the hedgehog should have awakened from hibernation. This easily recognisable mammal is nocturnal, spending its days sleeping under bushes or thick shrubs, only appearing at night to forage in woodland and farmland for caterpillars, earthworms and slugs.

Where to Walk in April

IN SOUTHERN COUNTIES, daffodils may be past their best in April, but further north they're at their finest in this month. Visit the Lake District and walk beside Ullswater, which inspired Wordsworth's immortal ode to the daffodil, or beside Rydal Water; by the church at Rydal is a field of daffodils planted by the poet himself.

DAFFODILS SHOULD ALSO be flourishing in the Yorkshire Dales, some of the finest walking country in England. Having wandered in Wensleydale or Swaledale and seen the daffodils and new lambs, have a go at one of the Three Peaks of Yorkshire, Whernside, Penyghent or Ingleborough. Whernside, the highest, is reachable on an easy day's circular walk from Ribblehead station, this walk also passes right underneath the remarkable Ribblehead Viaduct.

FOR A CLOSER encounter with the Yorkshire Dales, try the 96 mile Dales Way (not a national trail), which runs from Leeds to Windermere past Ilkley, Bolton Abbey, Grassington and Dent – a lovely mixture of riverside and upland walking, generally very easy.

IF THE SIGHT of daffodils by Ullswater has given you a taste for the Lake District, try walking the Cumbria Way. Though this isn't a national trail it runs for 70 stunning miles from Ulverston to Carlisle via some of Lakeland's loveliest scenery including Coniston, Dungeon Ghyll and Rosthwaite.

April

FOR A TASTE of the Lake District and Yorkshire Dales combined, there's the stunning 192-mile Coast to Coast between St Bees and Robin Hood's Bay. The walk was the brainchild of Alfred Wainwright and although still not an official long-distance route, is a marvellous and challenging expedition.

THOUGH THE DAFFODILS may be on their way out in the south, blossoms and bluebells are very much in. There's sure to be a bluebell wood near you. Take a walk in a bluebell wood where you may also enjoy the fragrance of wild garlic. Two particularly fine places to wander through bluebells in the southern half of Britain are Chawton Park Wood near Alton in Hampshire which is close to Chawton, Jane Austen's village, and Ebbor Gorge near Wells, Somerset, where besides bluebells in the ash woodland you'll find wood anemone and dog's mercury carpeting the woodland floor.

EASTER IS MOST likely to fall in April and there will invariably be a full moon in the week prior to Easter Day. A clear night with a full moon is the best time to undertake a night walk and go star-spotting – and possibly hedgehog spotting!

April Wisdom

APRIL WEATHER CAN be particularly unpredictable. The forecasters don't always get it right, especially during unsettled spells. Bear in mind also that long-range forecasts are notoriously unreliable, especially those found in the sensationalist tabloid press – pay no attention to them if you're planning when and where to walk.

THESE PIECES OF weather lore may assist, although they aren't foolproof.

'RAIN BEFORE SEVEN, fair before eleven.' – Unless the depression bringing the rain is very deep, it is rare for it to rain for more than 4 hours at a stretch in Great Britain.

'RED SKY AT night, shepherd's delight, red sky in the morning, shepherd's warning.' – Red sky may be indicative either of a weather front that's just passed or one that's approaching and bringing rain with it.

SADLY TWO OTHER pieces of weather lore – 'Oak before ash, we'll have a splash, ash before oak, we'll have a soak' and 'when swallows fly high, the weather will be dry' have no basis in meteorological fact. Indeed with climate change, the oak now routinely comes into leaf more quickly than the ash.

April

WHEN PLANNING A linear walk during a spell of unsettled windy weather, try to ensure your direction of travel means you have the wind on your back. Walking straight into a strong wind can make the task very much more demanding. Weather forecasts routinely state wind direction as well as speed.

IF CAUGHT OUT by wet weather in April and you're walking in ploughed clay soil, clay is much more likely to stick to your boots in great lumps, making walking much more of an effort. Get rid of the worst with the aid of a stick and lots of thick wet grass. It may help to kick an imaginary football – this will loosen the biggest lumps.

AS YOUR LATE spring and summer holiday walking adventures get closer, take the opportunity now to fine-tune your planning. Use the Internet to your fullest advantage: for instance, check availability of amenities such as buses, shops and pubs you may be seeking to use, and check tide times for walks where high tide will delay progress.

Notes

1
....

2
....

3
....

4
....

5
....

6
....

7
....

8
....

9
....

10
....

11
....

12
....

13
....

14
....

April

15
....

16
....

17
....

18
....

19
....

20
....

21
....

22
....

23
....

24
....

25
....

26
....

27
....

28
....

29
....

30
....

May

Landscape

FOR THE WALKER, May is a wonderful month: lots of sunshine and warmth, long days, and the countryside bursting into life with colour at every turn: the green of the fresh leaves and a profusion of whites, yellows, purples and pinks. Those 50 shades of winter grey seem like another lifetime ago.

INDEED TEMPERATURES IN the very high 20s Celsius in May are not uncommon, May 1989 and May 2012 being good examples. May produces plenty of sunshine, on average 152 hours in western Scotland (compared with just 18 in January) and three times as much sun on the south coast as in January. Southern England is generally frost-free by May.

RAIN IS WELL down too. It does rain sometimes in May – Alan Plowright reflects on the Fellsman challenge walk across the peaks and dales of North Yorkshire in that month: 'Eight body-destroying climbs I had made – and not one solitary view had I had in return.' But on average there will be just seven and a half rain days in southern England this month, and there will, in western Scotland, be less than a third of the amount of rain it suffers in January. So with less rain, more sun and more warmth, it really is a great month to be walking!

FOR THOSE SEEKING to enjoy some Scottish Highland scenery, there's now ample daylight to enjoy it. Sunrise in the north of Scotland will be at 5.15 a.m. at the beginning of the month, and before 4.30 a.m. by the end of the month.

'NE'ER CAST A clout till May be out.' – Commonly misunderstood as meaning one should continue to wrap up warm till the end of the month. But the May referred to here is in fact another name for the hawthorn, whose beautiful fragrant milky blossom appears in this month, to stunning effect particularly on rolling chalk downland.

IF YOU'RE WALKING in grassland, watch for orchids. May sees a number of orchids come into bloom, including the early purple, green-winged, early spider and early marsh, especially in moister habitats. The flowers of the early marsh and green-winged orchid can range from flesh pink to white to rose-purple.

MAY IS WITHOUT doubt the best month to be walking along our lanes. The verges will be rich with cow parsley as well as buttercups, daisies and dandelions, and the adjoining fields will be a rolling pageant of sparkling yellow as the oilseed rape flowers during this month. (Though hay fever sufferers beware!)

EVEN IF THE winter has been hard, deciduous trees including alder, hazel, elm, hornbeam and sycamore should now be fully in leaf, and a sunlit walk in beech or oak woods will be a joy as each tree shows off its fresh, sparkling green attire. In deciduous woodland you may also find the stinkhorn, unusual among fungi for its appearance in spring rather than in autumn.

May

ANOTHER ATTRACTIVE BLOSSOM to watch for in May is that of the elder, a common wayside, hedgerow and woodland plant, producing flat-topped umbels of white flowers, and you can also admire the beautiful columns of purple on chestnut trees.

OTHER WOODLAND PLANTS in flower in May include the yellows of pimpernel and common cow-wheat, while in the south, dry woodlands will see the white bell-shaped flowers of Solomon's seal, and in woodlands across England and Wales you may see the yellow flowers of the yellow archangel.

MAY IS THE best time of year to walk in grassland and meadows because of the number of wild plants in flower. Arguably the most distinctive and common wild meadow flower to be seen in May (though less common in Scotland) is the cowslip, with small orange-yellow flowers growing on long stalks.

AMONG THE MANY other grass and meadow flowers you will see in May are the yellow and orange flowers of the bird's foot trefoil; the yellow flowers of the meadow vetchling; the pinkish-purple flowers of the red clover; the creamy-white flowers of the white clover; the white, pink and blue flowers of the common milkwort; the yellow flowers of the wild radish; the brilliant white and yellow oxeye daisy; the bright blue flowers of viper's bugloss and the sheep's bit scabious.

May

IF YOU UNDERTAKE a coastal walk in May, watch out for the greenish-white flowers of the sea sandwort, the yellow star-shaped flowers of the biting stonecrop on sand dunes and shingle, and the lovely white five-petalled flowers of the sea campion on cliffs or stable shingle ridges.

I REMEMBER THE early May walk from the Lizard to Helford: clear blue skies and soft sunshine turning each cove into a crescent of gold. Thatched cottages at Cadgwith where the merest flicker of wind rippled across the boats moored in its harbour, the veritable tunnel of cow parsley and hawthorn on the approach to Coverack, the riot of wild flowers on the fringes of the seemingly vertical cliff paths, the sense of having earned every velvety mouthful of Cornish ice cream at the cafe at Porthallow.

IF YOU'RE WALKING in moorland in May, among the swathes of heather you may find the small pink bell-shaped flowers of the cowberry which appear in this month, widespread on moors in northern Britain, and the yellow four-petalled flowers of the tormentil, widespread on heaths as well as moors and acid grassland across Britain.

Wildlife

ALTHOUGH MANY WOULD associate butterflies with high summer, May is the peak time for the pearl-bordered fritillary butterfly, while the splendidly-named Duke of Burgundy butterfly can be found by walkers in chalk and limestone grassland or downland, and the migratory red admiral may also make an appearance, having travelled from France or Spain.

SIMILARLY, WHILE DRAGONFLIES and damselflies may seem like summer creatures, the hairy dragonfly can be seen by walkers from early May, and most large red damselflies appear this month also, being found on ponds, ditches, canals and bogs. Other species such as common blue and azure also begin to emerge during the month. If you walk in southern heathland you may see damselflies being trapped by the sticky hairs of the insectivorous sundew plant.

A NUMBER OF migrant birds will arrive back on the shores of Britain during this month, and birdwatching walkers in open country across southern England should look out in particular for the hobby – a falcon with a distinctive orange patch beneath its tail.

ANOTHER IMPRESSIVE MAY arrival is the honey buzzard, to be found in mature woodland and large undisturbed forests. While there may be fewer than 100 pairs breeding in Britain, mainly in the New Forest, Forest of Dean and woodlands in Wales, global warming may cause their numbers to increase.

May

IF YOU ARE particularly fortunate on your walks in May you could see the first dormice of the year, following their awakening from hibernation. The dormouse will have woven a tiny nest from bark and leaves and will have curled up here for up to seven months. Bats will also now have awoken but will be particularly elusive so consider a 'bat walk' (see below) if you want to see these amazing creatures.

VERY FORTUNATE RIVERSIDE walkers particularly in western and northern parts of Britain may see baby otters. Females produce a litter of two or three cubs from May onwards in a den by a riverbank, known as a holt. The Shetland Islands off north-eastern Scotland are a stronghold for otters and provide the best opportunities for observing them.

AND ONE CONSOLATION for those unable to escape to the May countryside in this beautiful month. If you're walking in a town or city you may observe stag beetles during this month, particularly in urban and suburban areas. Their main stronghold is London, where they are attracted by the capital's higher temperatures. The males have antlers on their heads, used for tussling with other males over females!

WITH BATS AND badgers having come out of hibernation, go on an organised bat walk with an expert guide or an organised visit to a badger sett, where again an expert guide can show you badgers without disturbing them.

Where to Walk in May

MAY IS RECKONED to be the best time of year to enjoy the dawn chorus. The ideal way to experience this is to venture into ancient woodland, away from other competing noise, but if that's not feasible, visit your nearest town or city park. Don't forget to set your alarm, though; dawn in May is well before 'normal' waking time for most.

TAKE A WALK in Glasdrum Woods, a nature reserve by Loch Creran, Argyll, boasting beautiful bluebell woods of ash and oak.

MAY IS AN excellent month for tackling part or all of a long-distance path. Most visitor attractions will have opened for the season, and you've the choice between going at half-term, if you're tied to school holidays, or avoiding half-term if you're not. The days are long and the weather is often settled and fine without the high summer temperatures and resulting heat hazes – so the clarity will be that much better.

THE SOUTH WEST Coast Path runs for 630 miles from Minehead in Somerset to Poole in Dorset, and embraces some of the finest coastal scenery in Britain, especially north Cornwall. You'll never complete the whole trail in a single two or three week expedition, but you'll enjoy taking different stretches at a time. Many stretches are at their best in spring.

May

Try Offa's Dyke Path, which runs for 178 miles from Sedbury near Chepstow in south Wales to Prestatyn on the Irish Sea coast of north Wales. This is one of the finest long-distance paths in Great Britain with its contrasts of gentle rolling scenery, rich in spring flowers and vegetation, and two impressive ranges of hills, the Black Mountains and the Clwydians.

The Pembrokeshire Coast Path, running for 177 miles from St Dogmaels to Amroth in south-west Wales, is another stunning coastal walk and, unlike the South West Coast Path, can comfortably be walked in a fortnight. The tiny cathedral city of St David's, the headlands of Strumble and Proud Giltar, and the astonishing Green Bridge of Wales, are just four of many highlights. The Pembrokeshire Coast Path has become a part of the 870-mile Wales Coast Path, now easily the longest waymarked route in Britain.

With the profusion of wild flowers which May brings, see how many different wild flowers you can find growing on a walk within a mile of your front door. But if you are able to go further afield in search of spring colour and some of the best wild flowers in Britain, venture off the Scottish shores to North and South Uist, or Ynys-hir, Ceredigion, a superb woodland reserve in the heart of Wales.

For more formal displays of May colour, see if any villages or towns near you are organising an open garden scheme where you can walk round one or more private gardens open to the public and enjoy displays of flowering plants that you may not find in the wild. Details should be available online (google National Garden Scheme) or at your nearest library.

May Wisdom

IF WALKING IN wilder terrain, as you will be if tackling, say, Offa's Dyke Path, you'll often be far from any amenities and it's essential that you carry food with you. Take what you enjoy eating but ensure it's rich in protein. Good choices include crispbread, cheese, dates, nuts, fruit (fresh or dried), Kendal Mint Cake, chocolate, and best of all, bananas – rich in potassium and providing slow-releasing energy. A simple snack of two bananas can keep you going for hours.

ALSO TAKE PLENTY to drink – water is best, juices are fine, but avoid carbonated drinks of any kind. You'll regret drinking them for several hours afterwards, and although this isn't strictly relevant to walking, they'll do your teeth no favours. Then again, neither will Kendal Mint Cake…

ASSUMING YOU HAVE the stamina, the secret of walking up to 20 miles or more, as you may be doing during the longer days, isn't so much walking fast as keeping moving with a minimum of stops. It's a good idea to study the route carefully in advance so you're not having to constantly stop to check the map once you get started.

TRAIN YOURSELF TO walk for 3 or 4 hours at a stretch without stops, except perhaps to enjoy a view or to catch your breath during a steep climb. Don't overlook the psychology of the early start, especially as early in the day is often the best time to observe wildlife. When you do stop, relax completely; find a spot out of the wind, lie flat on your back and just enjoy the moment.

May

WALKING LONG DISTANCES increases the risk of blisters. Blisters are usually not the result of walking too much but doing so in inadequate or badly fitting socks and/or shoes/boots, or allowing foreign matter to affect the foot. Prevention is better than cure so make sure not only that your footwear is dry and comfortable but you get rid of any foreign matter the moment you become aware of it, even if it means having to stop. Also make sure you've a first aid kit with you.

AT THE FIRST sign of blisters, stop and examine the foot. If the blister is small, make a hole in it, ideally pushing a sterilised needle through it from one side to another; take a tissue and squeeze the blister till all the fluid is out; and cover with a suitably sized cushioned plaster. Then examine your socks and boots for any other foreign matter before continuing.

MORE SEVERE BLISTERS should be protected by thick adhesive moleskin. Cut a hole in the moleskin, large enough to contain the blister, and apply it after treating the blister as above. Treat any product promising 'instant blister pain relief' with circumspection at best, but talk to other, experienced walkers about what helps them. Some walkers have found sheep's wool very effective!

COAST PATH WALKING inevitably entails some tramping along sand dunes and shingle which can at times seem like penance for sin. It's always worth shopping around for firmer patches of sand, or sections of shingle that support your feet rather than suck them in, in preference to trudging obstinately in a straight line.

Notes

1 ....

2 ....

3 ....

4 ....

5 ....

6 ....

7 ....

8 ....

9 ....

10 ....

11 ....

12 ....

13 ....

14 ....

May

15
....

16
....

17
....

18
....

19
....

20
....

21
....

22
....

23
....

24
....

25
....

26
....

27
....

28
....

29
....

30
....

31
....

June

Landscape

JUNE SEES THE transition from spring to summer. Laurie Lee recalling his June walk through Wiltshire in *As I Walked Out One Midsummer Morning*: 'High sulky summer sucked me towards it and I offered no resistance at all… I was oppressed by the velvety emptiness of the world and the swathes of soft grass I lay on…'

THE LONGEST DAY of the year is on 21 June, and the long hours of daylight in this month provide ample opportunity for early morning or late evening walks. During the last week of June sunset does not arrive until well after 10 p.m. in northern Scotland.

THE 24 JUNE is known as Midsummer Day. But in this context 'mid' is derived from the German meaning 'with', in other words, 'with summer' or 'the start of summer'. So don't be misled into thinking that temperatures will start to fall after 24 June. In fact temperatures will continue to rise steadily, and generally peak in early August.

INDEED NATURE CAN spring a chilly surprise in June. A number of cricket matches were disrupted by hail, sleet and snow on 2 June 1975. That said, the summer of 1975 was one of the hottest on record (and was followed by THE hottest and driest next year!)

June

AN IDEAL JUNE Lakeland day: up Helvellyn in the morning, out to a village tearoom on the fringes of the Lake District for sausage sandwiches made with home-baked bread... then back to Gatesgarth on the shores of Buttermere and an evening ascent of Haystacks, gazing from Wainwright's beloved summit towards Scotland at 7.30 in the evening, secure in the knowledge of ample daylight to see us safely home again...

FOR WOODLAND OR hedgerow walkers in southern Britain, June sees a number of trees and shrubs in flower, including the small, white flowers of the wild service tree, the white wild pear blossom, the pink white blossom from the crab apple tree, clusters of white flowers from the dogwood, and white flowers from the guelder rose.

ONE OF THE most instantly recognisable flowering trees for the walker is the rhododendron, and in June it's at its very best. You can enjoy particularly fine displays of this shrub in the Ardnamurchan region of western Scotland, but it thrives in damp woodland throughout Great Britain and its large pinkish-red flowers which appear this month, set against its lush green leaves, provide a breathtaking sight for woodland walkers.

OTHER WOODLAND PLANTS in flower in June include the yellow flowers of the tutsan in southern and western Britain; the white flowers of the common wintergreen in northern Britain; yellow flowers of the wood sage and goldenrod; the purple white flowers of the wood vetch and, in England and Wales, the betony with its reddish-purple flowers in dense spikes.

IF YOU LOOK carefully while walking in deciduous woodlands in June you may see some dryad's saddle, an often very large fungus which forms tiered brackets on deciduous trees, particularly the ash and elm, and remains till September. It has a creamy, scaly upper surface while its lower surface is porous and greyish white.

WITH TEMPERATURES RISING, a walk by the sea or on the cliffs is tempting, and there are a number of coastal plants which flower in June, including the pale lilac or white flowers of the sea rocket on sandy coasts; small white flowers of wild celery in southern English coastal grassland; the white flowers of the English stonecrop on sea cliffs and, on southern and western coasts, the pink and white striped flowers of the sea bindweed on the dunes and the small yellow flowers of rock samphire in the shingle.

THE GRASS VERGES continue to be havens of beautiful wild flowers in June, often providing better displays than in farmed fields as they are safe from herbicides. As you walk along country lanes in this month, look out for hogweed, similar in appearance to cow parsley, the reddish-purple rosebay willowherb, red valerian and yellow agrimony.

IF YOU'RE WALKING in the moors in June, you'll find colour provided in northern and western moorland by the purplish-red flowers of bell heather; in peaty soils by the bright yellow flowers of the bog asphodel and in upland regions of northern Britain, the delicate white five-petalled flowers of the cloudberry.

But walking in open grassland in June offers a wealth of wild plants in flower including the soft greyish cylindrical hairs of hare's foot clover; the yellow flowers of lady's bedstraw; the bright reddish-purple of bloody cranesbill (particularly stunning in the Peak District); the pinkish-purple thyme flowers; the pink flowers of the common centaury; the white flowers of the burnet saxifrage and in England, the yellow flowers of the creeping Jenny and rough hawkbit, and the purple flowers of the musk thistle.

More orchids are appearing in June including the common spotted orchid and the greater butterfly orchid. The greater butterfly orchid is found in woodland and grassland and has greenish-white flowers with long spurs and yellow pollen sacs, while the common spotted orchid has spikes which may be of pale pink, pale purple or white, and is both a widespread and common grassland plant.

While poppies are most commonly associated with Remembrance Day in November, this easily recognised flower, with its four papery red petals, comes into flower in June and is a common sight particularly on arable and waste ground. The red of the common poppy contrasts with the yellow of the Welsh poppy, which is native to damp woods, not only in Wales, but also south-west England.

Wildlife

P. G. WODEHOUSE once wrote of a
golfer that he 'missed putts because
of the uproar of the butterflies in adjoining meadows.'
But any countryside walker on a hot sunny June day
will be aware, among the hedgerows, of the noise
of bees and other insects encouraged there by the
tangle of diverse vegetation. Listen particularly for the
distinctive sounds of the cricket and the grasshopper, a
key part of their courtship displays.

BY JUNE, THE seabird colonies round the coastal
headlands and offshore islands of Britain are reaching
their peak, and coastal walkers in northern and
western Scotland may be rewarded with the sight of
thousands of such birds including puffins, fulmars,
guillemots and skuas gathering to breed having
overwintered at sea.

WE SAW HOW many damselflies and dragonflies appear
in May, but late in June the rest of the approximately
20 kinds of damselflies in Britain arrive, including the
willow emerald and dainty damselflies and the banded
and beautiful demoiselles. The demoiselles, with their
bright metallic green bodies, can be found
around rivers and streams and are often
mistaken for dragonflies because of their
large size.

June

THIS IS THE best time of year for walkers on chalk and limestone grasslands in southern Britain to observe the beautiful chalk downland butterflies. The blues are among the most striking, particularly the brightly-coloured common blue and the sparkling Adonis blue, while you can also spot several species of 'brown' butterfly including marbled white, small heath and grayling, as well as small copper, meadow brown and hedge brown.

ONE PARTICULARLY BEAUTIFUL migrant species which has increased dramatically in Britain in recent years, and which is now a regular sight from late spring, is the hummingbird hawk-moth. These originate in Spain and north Africa, and flit from one flower to another on whirring wings and although they are insects they might easily be confused with real hummingbirds.

JOHN HILLABY, NEARING the conclusion of his end-to-end walk across Britain, recalls reaching the head of Loch Quoich in western Scotland one June morning and observing half a dozen fawns 'who scampered about like lambs, butting and frolicking, racing up and down hillocks, often falling flat on their noses.'

Where to Walk in June

IF YOU'RE WANTING to bag some serious mountain tops, June is the time to go, if your circumstances allow. The days are as long as they ever get in Great Britain, you have the best chance of fine dry weather and the school holidays haven't yet started, meaning there are fewer people about and accommodation will be less expensive.

CLIMB SOME WAINWRIGHTS – the mountains and fells in the Lake District documented and mapped by the great walker and illustrator Alfred Wainwright. Climb to Scafell Pike, the peak of England, try one or more of the other Big Four in Lakeland – Scafell, Skiddaw (the easiest of the four) or Helvellyn, all over 3,000 ft high, or have a go at that most distinctive Lakeland peak, Great Gable, just 51 ft short of the 3,000 but providing a superb walking experience.

IF THAT'S TOO big an ask trample on Wainwright's ashes on his beloved Haystacks. Bag several peaks in one day with one of the Lake District's horse shoe circuits – Mosedale, Newlands or Fairfield – or pick off the Langdale Pikes: Pike o'Stickle with its pepper pot top, Harrison Stickle and Pavey Ark.

CONQUER THE DADDY of all mountains in Britain, Ben Nevis near Fort William in Scotland. The climb from Glen Nevis Youth Hostel just outside Fort William, easily reached by bus from the town, requires no mountaineering skills, just patience. Allow a full day for the trip there and back – the average time taken to ascend is roughly 3 hours.

To GET TO Fort William in the first place, walk the 95-mile West Highland Way from Milngavie, a terrific journey, initially beside Loch Lomond and then across Rannoch Moor. Allow six or seven days – it's strenuous in places particularly beside Loch Lomond where the path is often very rough, but the views across the loch are astonishing,

IF BEN NEVIS whets your appetite for Munros (Scottish mountains exceeding 3,000 ft) visit the Trossachs in central Scotland and have a go at Ben Lomond (974 m) or Ben More (1,174 m). You may become an obsessive Munro bagger but remember there are 282 of them in Scotland.

IN WALES THERE'S Snowdonia, including the challenge of Snowdon, the peak of the Principality. You don't need to be a climbing expert; the easiest way up is the Pyg track; a fair tramp but certainly not technically difficult, unless the weather is particularly bad. Then move to the Brecon Beacons with its magnificent trio of Pen-y-fan, Cribyn and Corn Du, easily accomplished in a single expedition.

IF YOU DON'T feel up to tackling a Munro, why not use June to bag a Marilyn? Marilyns are hills with an overall drop of 492 ft (150 m) on each side, and there are 2,009 in Great Britain. By definition there will be many Marilyns in even comparatively low-lying parts of Britain, several of them will be easy to climb and they frequently offer tremendous views. Google Marilyns and you're on your way.

June Wisdom

IF YOU'RE WALKING in the mountains in June but are unsure how much you can manage in a day, Naismith's Rule will help: allow one hour for every 3 miles measured on the map, plus an additional hour for every 2,000 ft climbed. The distance climbed isn't the highest point reached but the sum total of all the ascents. This formula assumes good conditions; extra time should be allowed for bad weather, difficulties in route-finding, heavy packs and refreshment breaks.

WHEN MOUNTAIN WALKING, remember the Mountain Code: don't tackle anything beyond your training or experience; ensure your equipment is sound; know what rescue facilities are available; know how to apply first aid both to yourself and your companions if any; avoid going alone unless you're experienced; leave word of your route and your anticipated return time and report your return; and make sure you know how to read maps and operate a compass or GPS device.

YOUR WORST ENEMY as a mountain or fell walker is mist or fog which can descend suddenly and cause you to lose all sense of direction. In such conditions possession of, and ability to use, a compass or GPS device is essential. Otherwise, if you're caught in mist or fog it's best to stay put and either wait for it to clear or call for assistance rather than take a chance and put yourself in danger. What looks like a seductively clear rocky path could be leading you over a sheer cliff edge.

WHEN CLIMBING A very steep section of hill or mountain, consider zigzagging – say one or two steps at 45 degrees and then 45 degrees in the opposite direction. When possible, put the whole of the sole of the foot down on firm ground, avoiding toe or heel holds.

WHEN WALKING DOWN a particularly steep section, allow the legs to bend slightly at the knee so the body isn't jarred each time you place your foot on the ground. If the ground isn't too rough, you could consider running downhill in a skipping motion taking very short steps, turning 45 degrees every few yards, but watch for trip hazards (see below).

MAKE A CONSCIOUS effort to pick your feet up towards the end of the day. Tiredness may lead to a dragging of the feet and/or lack of vigilance for the ground below which in turn can result in tripping or stumbling. In rocky terrain this could cause cuts and bruises at best and fractures at worst.

HEED THE WORDS of Alfred Wainwright, 'Don't forget to watch where you are putting your feet... Fellwalking accidents happen only to those who walk clumsily. If you want to look at a view, stop, look, and only then move on.'

Notes

1
....

2
....

3
....

4
....

5
....

6
....

7
....

8
....

9
....

10
....

11
....

12
....

13
....

14
....

June

15
....

16
....

17
....

18
....

19
....

20
....

21
....

22
....

23
....

24
....

25
....

26
....

27
....

28
....

29
....

30
....

July

Landscape

THE BEGINNING OF July sees almost 18 hours of daylight for walkers between sunrise and sunset in Scotland, the sun rising at 4.15 a.m. and setting at 10.10 p.m. In southern England it's still light before 5 a.m., sunset not arriving until gone 9.15 p.m. In essence, the first few days of July are only shorter than the longest day by a minute or two.

ALTHOUGH IT MIGHT be thought that following the longest day the nights would start to draw in, that isn't the case; in the month between 21 June and 21 July in London, only 26 minutes of daylight will be lost at the start of the day and 17 minutes at the day's end. It's only as we reach August that the drawing-in properly accelerates. So if you need plenty of daylight for your walks, July will work as well as June.

NOT ONLY DAYLIGHT but temperatures peak in July in many parts of Britain. July is the warmest month of the year in parts of northern England with an average maximum temperature of 21.1 degrees Celsius, and it's also the warmest in north-west Scotland with an average maximum of 18.4.

July

How reliable is the proverb that if it rains on St Swithun's Day, 15 July, it will rain for the next 40 days while if it is fine that day, it will be dry for the following 40 days? Sadly for walkers who are enthusiasts of weather lore, there hasn't been a single period of 40 days following 15 July which has been entirely dry or seen rain every day.

There is an element of truth in the proverb though. It's thought to be about mid-July that the jet stream which controls our weather settles down, its position over the ensuing weeks either allowing warm air to feed in from the Continent, or bringing Atlantic weather systems with consequently unsettled, cooler and wet conditions.

But all that said, July is also generally the driest and sunniest month of the year and for that reason good news for walkers. Bognor Regis in West Sussex enjoys an average of 252 hours sunshine every July (more than 8 hours every day) – comfortably more than any other month of the year. It is not unknown for there to be over 350 hours of sunshine in July.

July is generally a dry month. In parts of southern England there are on average just six and a half days and 40 mm of rain, significantly less than any other month.

DRY CONDITIONS MEAN that normally testing terrain becomes manageable. Simon Armitage recalls the Pennine Way in July following a very dry spring and early summer: 'The higher ground, usually a morass of liquefied peat and standing water, is bone dry.'

FOR WALKERS WHO like sweet treats, both strawberries and raspberries will be available in mid-July; some strawberries may be found in the wild, in dry grassland, but for a guaranteed supply of both fruit you may want to walk to a countryside pick-your-own farm. Both fruits are a rich source of dietary fibre and being high in antioxidants may help avoid inflammations, heart disease and certain types of cancer.

I RECALL THE Peddars Way, Norfolk on a Sunday morning in late July: yet another in a sequence of fine sunny days, a long, straight, unerring track across rolling farmland, adjoining cornfields bulging with poppies, a riot of butterflies attending my every step and ladybirds nestling on the lush path-side vegetation, the coast getting nearer with each step, the prospect of tea and ice cream in Ringstead encouraging me on.

SEVERAL GRASSLAND PLANTS come into flower in July including the yellow flowers of the slender St John's Wort and perennial sow-thistle; the pink flowers of the restharrow; the purple or white flowers of the marsh thistle; the yellow flowers of the ploughman's spikenard and the pale pink flowers of the musk mallow in England and Wales; the blue or mauve flowers of the field gentian in northern Britain and the pinkish flowers of the marjoram in southern England. And among the bracken of the New Forest, watch for the beautiful pink flowers of the wild gladiolus.

COASTAL WALKERS WILL be rewarded with the appearance of the yellow, purple or blue flowers of the sea aster on cliffs or saltmarshes; the white flowers of the sea kale on shingle and sand; the blue flowers of the sea holly on shingle and sand in England and Wales; the yellow flowers of the fennel in grassy places close to the shore in England and Wales. Wormwood, an inoffensive and very aromatic perennial with its stiff spikes of small yellowish flowers, can also be seen in England and Wales.

WALKERS SEEKING THE shade of woodland on a hot day, the broad leaves of the deciduous trees providing an umbrella of sparkling green, may find a number of woodland plants in flower including the purple flowers of the greater burdock in England and Wales, the white flowers of the wild angelica and the (hopefully for hay fever sufferers, not prophetically named) white flowers of the sneezewort.

Wildlife

WITH SUMMER REACHING its peak, adventurous walkers travelling to one of our more remote coastlines or offshore islands may be rewarded with sightings of whales, porpoises, dolphins and sharks. Bottlenose dolphins can be seen in the Moray Firth east of Inverness and in Cardigan Bay off the Welsh coast. Although many stay far out to sea, others can be seen from the shore.

WHEREVER YOU ARE walking in July, listen out for the skylark, whose song, heard in high summer across Britain, has been described as a 'tumultuous outpouring of notes' (Stephen Moss). They can be found in a remarkably large range of habitats from city parks to offshore islands.

WHILE ON FOOT in Scotland in summer, watch for ospreys. Since 1954 these birds of prey, with their long brown-topped wings, have nested beside Loch Garten, near Aviemore close to the Speyside Way long-distance path, and they can be seen throughout much of Scotland, as well as in areas of Wales and by Rutland Water in the heart of England.

THE LONG DAYS of July provide the best opportunity for sightings by walkers of a group of predatory mammals named mustelids, including the stoat, weasel, pine marten and polecat. Though they are all primarily nocturnal, the long hours of daylight during the summer months mean they are often visible around dawn and dusk.

STOATS AND WEASELS are widespread across Britain but the polecat is generally confined to Wales and the pine marten to forests in the northern and western Highlands of Scotland. Young polecats weigh just 10 grams at birth and will appear in the open with their mothers in July; there may be as many as ten in one litter.

THE HEIGHT OF summer is the best time for walkers to observe dragonflies, including the chaser, skimmer and common darter and the huge emperor which is one of Britain's largest insects. Thousands of them may be found on wetlands such as the Norfolk Broads.

A WALK BY the sea on a hot July day offers an excellent opportunity for exploring rock pools at low tide. If you look carefully and are prepared to be patient you may be rewarded with such fish as gobies, blennies, shrimps and sea anemones, all of which are widespread around the coasts of Britain.

NOT ALL WILDLIFE is welcome for July walkers. John Merrill walking near Crinan in western Scotland on 12 July 1978 recalled: 'The hot weather ensured that the clegs had a field day... [they] persistently buzzed in my ears and nose and crawled over my bare arms.'

Where to Walk in July

THE IDEAL ANTIDOTE to the beating of the sun is a walk in woodland. Woods will provide welcome shade on a boiling hot day. Check the map to find your nearest woodland. Where on an Ordnance Survey Explorer map the wood is shaded in lighter green, it means the whole wood is access land and you can walk anywhere within it at will, without having to keep to paths.

TRY A WALK on one of our offshore islands. Ferry services will generally be at their peak in the height of summer, and the wildlife will be exceptional. For instance red squirrel and kingfisher on Brownsea off Poole, seal colonies on the Farne Islands off Northumberland, and puffins on the Isle of May off Anstruther, Fife in Scotland.

FOR A NOT-TOO-CHALLENGING long-distance walk, follow the 50 miles of the Peddars Way between Great Massingham and Hunstanton in Norfolk, with its profusion of wild flowers, birds and butterflies, and a refreshing seaside stroll at the end.

DRAGONFLIES ARE SYNONYMOUS with summer. So take a walk on Thursley Common near Farnham in Surrey, regarded as the premier site for dragonflies, with over 20 different species to be found. While there, watch beneath your feet for adders, while overhead you may spot woodlarks, tree pipits or Dartford warblers.

ANOTHER CREATURE CLOSELY associated with high summer is the butterfly. So what better month to walk the South Downs Way, the 99-mile walk from Winchester in Hampshire to Eastbourne in East Sussex? You will cross grassy chalk downland, observing such beauties as the Adonis blue and chalkhill blue, and enjoying magnificent views to the Weald and the sea.

IF YOU WANT to escape the heat of southern England, try walking part or all of Hadrian's Wall Path, a national trail which runs for 84 miles from Newcastle to the Solway Firth in Cumbria, through the heart of the Northumberland National Park, tracing the defensive wall dating back 2,000 years and of which much evidence remains today. The scenery, particularly round Housesteads – arguably the most famous fort on the wall – is magnificent, with extensive views across Northumberland.

TAKE A WALK in the Forest of Dean in Gloucestershire, 110 square kilometres of mixed woodland and one of the surviving ancient woodlands of England. There's a huge variety of deciduous and evergreen trees including oak, beech, sweet chestnut, Weymouth pine, Norway spruce, larch and Douglas fir, one of the tallest types of tree in Britain. Further north, Sherwood Forest in Nottinghamshire offers a 450 acre country park with some of the oldest trees in Europe and, of course, associations with the legend of Robin Hood.

July Wisdom

WHILE HOT JULY days will encourage
you out into the countryside, the effect
of hot weather on the body shouldn't be
underestimated. If the body gets too hot it
naturally produces sweat. Like shivering, sweating is
to be avoided because the body is wasting energy in an
attempt to regulate its temperature.

REDUCE BODY HEAT by taking things more gently in
hot weather and resting during the hottest part of the
day. Remember too that during the hottest days, the
mornings will always be less hot than the afternoons,
so try to get as much walking as you can done in the
early hours of the day. Wildlife is often at its best just
after daybreak.

EVEN ON THE hottest days you can avoid thirst by
drinking water from the moment you start your
day's walk and continuing to drink little and often
throughout your walk. If you wait till you're thirsty,
you're already dehydrated and it's too late. It's
impossible to imagine how bad thirst is until you
experience it for yourself.

DON'T SQUANDER PRECIOUS funds on buying bottled
water. Take plenty of water with you and top up your
empty water bottles from the tap whenever you
get the chance. No cafe at which you stop
for refreshment should refuse to help in
this regard – provided you buy something!

Never put your reliance on water from rivers and streams. Such water may be polluted and result in sickness and/or diarrhoea, ruining your walking holiday.

SUPPLEMENT YOUR WATER with occasional hot drinks but remember the cheapest teas and coffees are the ones in your Thermos. In a large village or town with a wide variety of hot drink options, it's the big chains which are paradoxically the most expensive. The best value is to be found in independent bakers' shops doing takeaway coffees and teas – to go with their home-made cakes and buns!

REMEMBER THAT WOODLAND shaded lighter green on Explorer maps is what's known as access land, in which you can walk at will without reference to paths. Open access land is also clearly delineated on Explorer maps.

BUT WHILE ACCESS land brings greater freedom to roam, particularly in woodland or on commons, it also brings greater responsibility. Especially if you're walking on land on which people depend for a living, remember the Countryside Code. In particular, leave things exactly as you find them: take nothing except photographs and leave nothing except your footprints on the ground.

Notes

1
....

2
....

3
....

4
....

5
....

6
....

7
....

8
....

9
....

10
....

11
....

12
....

13
....

14
....

July

15

16

17

18

19

20

21

22

23

24

25

26

27

28

29

30

31

August

Landscape

I RECALL THE walk from Fowey to Polperro on a hot sunny Sunday in early August: cloudless blue skies above Lantic Bay; a clear deserted path through the little trees and shrubs beyond Lansallos, the only sounds coming from the bell buoy and the ripple of the sea below; then Polperro, this hitherto solitary walker, just one more mouth to feed amongst the queues for take-home clotted cream and see-it-made toffee fudge.

IT'S IRONIC THAT whilst August may be the only month when schoolchildren, their parents and also those working in schools are able to have a proper holiday, it's not the best month to be out walking. Summer heat may have left grassland parched and burnt and the high temperatures August often attracts will not be good for walking long distances. That said, settled weather undoubtedly makes your walking adventures easier to plan and enjoy.

THOUGH AUGUST BRINGS us into late summer, this month claims all the heat records for Great Britain: all parts of Great Britain have recorded temperatures in the 30s Celsius during this month with southern England recording over 38 degrees on one occasion.

August

DAYTIME AUGUST HEAT can bring compensations in the form of being interspersed with balmy still nights, and a night walk in such conditions may yield a huge variety of moths, many of which are nocturnal, among them the yellow underwings. A moth trap or just a white sheet and bright torch will help identify them.

OF COURSE, PERSISTENT dry weather has benefits for the walker. Path surfaces will be firm, regardless of the type of soil, and heavy boots can be discarded in favour of trainers. Even active streams may be fordable, while walks which might take whole days can be completed in a few hours.

MY TRAVERSE OF the Black Mountains on Offa's Dyke Path one dusty August Monday is a case in point: a supposedly challenging walk, often treacherous underfoot, reduced to an easy canter because of the fine dry conditions, the cairns almost redundant as the dusty path sped surely across the heathery plateau, climaxing with Hay Bluff and the ground falling away to the haven of Hay-on-Wye on the far side of the mountains.

BUT PAYBACK WAS to follow three days later, the fierce late summer heat pummelling me as I negotiated the switchback section of Offa's Dyke Path between Knighton and Montgomery. But sweet relief was to follow further up the path with the cool refreshing woodland around World's End and the delight of discovering a still active stream.

AUGUST IS THE best month to see ling, often known simply as heather, in flower, and our heaths and moors, from the Cornish heath on the Lizard peninsula at one end of the country to Breckland in Norfolk and the North York Moors at the other, will be a riot of purple.

MANY OF US remember from our schooldays the hymn 'All Things Bright and Beautiful' and the reference to 'The purple headed mountain; the river running by.' In late summer on the Speyside Way in north east Scotland this vision becomes a reality, the lofty heather-clad slopes between Ballindalloch and Grantown contrasting with the serene flow of the Spey.

THE NEW FOREST, beside its fine display of heather broken up by the yellow of gorse, is the best place in Britain to see the coral necklace, beautiful white flowers on reddish stems, which are at their finest in August, thriving on the marginal soils round the shallow pools of the forest.

ARGUABLY THE MOST familiar species of toadstool, the fly agaric, appears in August. These toadstools will always be found growing on heaths and commons where the birch tree, with which the agaric is associated, is found. They have distinctive bright red caps dotted with flecks of white.

AUGUST SEES THE harvesting of fields by crop farmers, so be prepared to give way to harvesters crossing your path, and perhaps walk round the fields rather than over. But there is good news – the practice of stubble burning, once so common in late summer and a real hazard for walkers, has become effectively illegal across England and Wales since the 1990s.

EVENING WALKERS TAKE note: August brings the first real signs that the year is on the wane as far as daylight is concerned. It's now getting darker more quickly; whilst sunset is just half an hour earlier in London at the end of July than at the start, August sees the loss of a whole hour of evening daylight, sunset being at 8.49 p.m. on the 1st and 7.49 p.m. on the 31st.

Wildlife

JOHN MERRILL IN the Torridon region of Scotland recalled the richness of bird life there in August: 'I had seen a variety of birds during the day.' He reported seeing a red-throated diver, a golden eagle, a red-breasted merganser, cormorants, buzzards, a merlin, a wren, gannets and eider ducks...

BUT WHILST WALKING along the west coast of Scotland he was unable to escape the attention of one less welcome summer visitor to north and west Scotland, the Highland midge, which can be a serious nuisance to walkers: 'Midges descended in the morning and attacked me ferociously as I packed the tent away.'

WALKING AMONGST THE sandy heaths of Dorset, Hampshire and Surrey in August, you may be fortunate enough to see a sand lizard or smooth snake, the latter preying on the former. The smooth snake is slender grey-brown and might well be mistaken for an adder, while the sand lizard is dressed with distinctive green flanks. The preferred habitat of both is a sunny bank on heathland where they like to bask.

THE MOORLANDS SURROUNDING the Cairngorms in north-east Scotland are at their finest in August when the flowering of the heather is at its peak. The moors are home to red deer and red grouse, the red deer living on the high tops in summer with their newborn calves before moving into the glens in winter.

August

IF YOU'RE WALKING in August you may notice the absence of birdsong and far fewer birds actually out in the open. Trevor Jones wrote in his 1970s 'Out And About' column in a Surrey church magazine in mid-August: 'The usual end-of-the-breeding season silence has fallen on our bird front with only the robin keeping up any pretence at song, although alarm and food calls persist.' You will be more likely to hear the low hum of bumblebees in the woods and the hedgerows.

BIRDS ARE IN fact hiding away in order to avoid predators as they moult into fresh plumage in order to prepare themselves for winter. In particular, ducks' feathers will have become worn after raising their new young, and during August, when food is plentiful, they will be acquiring a brand new set of bright feathers.

OTHER BIRDS SUCH as warblers and flycatcher, hiding in the forest canopy, will have an even more practical reason for acquiring new feathers: to ensure they're in the best condition for their long journey south to the African savannah. Migration is nearing: you may see swallows starting to gather on telephone wires, readying themselves for their departure, from time to time swooping off as though rehearsing for it.

AUGUST AND SEPTEMBER are the peak times for breeding of the harvest mouse, a farmland creature found mainly in southern Britain. Seen in crop fields, long grass and hedgerows, they are easily identifiable with their yellowish brown coat and white underparts, and can produce as many as eight young.

Where to Walk in August

WITH THE OFTEN high August temperatures, particularly early in the month, relax and chill with a riverside or canalside walk. Check out your nearest waterway – there's one near you.

THE THAMES PATH National Trail, 184 miles from the source of the river in Gloucestershire to the Thames Barrier in London, is Britain's best inland waterside walk – a journey on foot beside the Thames from source to flood barrier. Contrast the lush and surprisingly remote water meadows along the early miles, the towpaths in the leafy London suburbs and the new walkways beside the impressive contemporary developments of central and east London.

THE GREAT GLEN Way National Trail, 73 miles from Fort William to Inverness in the Scottish Highlands, runs alongside the Caledonian Canal or lochs, including Loch Ness, for virtually all of its length. It's a very undemanding walk, offering fabulous views to Ben Nevis, beautifully situated locks (sic) and the possibility of a sighting of Nessie!

THERE IS NOW an excellent choice of well-maintained canal walks. Try the 16 mile section of the Leeds and Liverpool Canal between Leeds and Bingley, or if you prefer something more rural, try the towpath of the Montgomery and Brecon Canal running for 30 miles between Brecon and Cwmbran in south Wales, or that of the Grantham Canal, a 33-mile walk between Grantham and Nottingham.

August

HEAD SOUTH-WESTWARDS FROM Exmoor to Dartmoor with its hills called tors – heather hillsides with stark rocky summits. Pick a sunny day and scale the summit of Dartmoor, High Willhays, which with its even more impressive neighbour Yes Tor is an easy day's walk from the town of Okehampton. High summer is also the best time of year to explore the blanket bogs on the Dartmoor plateau. Not only is it likely that the ground will be drier and easy to walk on, but you can enjoy the sight of the very distinctive cotton grass flowers among the heather, and also the migration of frogs and toads to the bog pools.

AUGUST IS PARTICULARLY suitable for walking in the Cairngorms National Park in north-east Scotland. The Speyside Way offers a generally easy walk in serious whisky country, with many 'purple-headed mountains' on show, but the higher Cairngorm slopes will usually be snow-free and thus more accessible. This part of Britain is fabulously rich in wildlife; look out for osprey, golden eagle, ptarmigan, buzzard, capercaillie, red deer, red squirrel, otter and wildcat.

AUGUST IS THE best month to visit the New Forest National Park in Hampshire. The forest is famed for its ponies but also supports large numbers of deer. Cattle and pigs roam freely in the forest, and you may also see adders. Not only are there some beautiful woodland walks but some charming small towns and villages such as Lymington, Buckler's Hard and Beaulieu, plus some tremendous coastal scenery round Hurst Castle, the nearest point of the mainland to the Isle of Wight.

August Wisdom

WHILE IT MAY be tempting to walk in a T-shirt and shorts in hot weather, this makes your skin more vulnerable to stings and scratches from nettles, thistles etc., but more seriously increases the risk of sunburn. Exercise makes sunburn more likely because perspiration tends to irritate the skin which has already been made tender by the sun. Sunburn comes on you almost unnoticed and can be very painful.

GUARD AGAINST THE risk of sunburn either by the use of sunblock which can be very expensive, or by wearing loose-fitting, long-sleeved tops and light trousers when out walking. Incidentally, windburn, which can affect you at any time of year, can make the face tender and crack the lips, so it's a good idea to guard against this by carrying soothing cream and lip salve.

WHEN THE WEATHER is both hot and unsettled, the risk of thunderstorms increases. The difficulty with storms is that they can be very isolated and even if they are forecast you may miss them altogether. Nonetheless, if it's clear that a storm is very near or imminent, better not to set out at all than take the risk.

IF A THUNDERSTORM strikes when you are out, seek the nearest escape route and try to get refuge in a building, a wholly enclosed shelter or a hard-topped vehicle. Avoid trees, exposed sheds, fences and poles, and on no account put up an umbrella or use your mobile phone.

IF YOU'VE NO shelter available in a storm, keep moving but avoid being the tallest object. If you find you are, crouch down with your feet together and your head tucked down. Don't lie flat on the ground and avoid standing in water. Let go of any exposed pointed metal items which may include walking poles.

ANOTHER HAZARD ASSOCIATED with being outside in hot weather is the risk of stings from bees or, more commonly, wasps which are plentiful at this time of year. Such stings are not generally dangerous and can be treated by washing the wound, applying ice to it and bandaging it. The best pain relief is ibuprofen which can be obtained over the counter.

THAT SAID, THERE may exceptionally be allergic reactions (anaphylaxis) to such a sting, when the body goes into shock and there are such symptoms as swelling, itching, breathing difficulties or stomach cramps. In such circumstances, seek medical help immediately.

Notes

1
....

2
....

3
....

4
....

5
....

6
....

7
....

8
....

9
....

10
....

11
....

12
....

13
....

14
....

August

15
....

16
....

17
....

18
....

19
....

20
....

21
....

22
....

23
....

24
....

25
....

26
....

27
....

28
....

29
....

30
....

31
....

September

Landscape

SEPTEMBER OFFERS THE best of all possible worlds for the walker: the August heat has receded, there are no extremes of heat, cold, wind or rain, the weather is generally more settled than in August and there's still plenty of daylight. Early in the month it is still light until 8 p.m. in northern Scotland and 7.45 p.m. in London.

HOWEVER THE NIGHTS are drawing in quickly and by the end of the month the sun will have set well over an hour earlier across Britain than at the start of the month. Everywhere there's a sharp fall in average maximum temperatures, by some 3 degrees Celsius, and, in western Scotland, a significant increase in monthly average rainfall.

I REMEMBER THE South West Coast Path between Worth Matravers and Studland in Dorset one baking hot September Saturday: summer's last fling – parched cliff grasses, the brightness of the sun seeming to add an even greater whiteness to the towering Old Harry rock stacks. Swanage teeming with visitors and swimmers; the nudists at Studland making even this scantily clad walker feel overdressed.

FOR THE COUNTRY walker in September, nature's great edible free gift, blackberries, are everywhere. Blackberries have one of the highest antioxidant levels of all fruits, and eating them brings a number of health benefits, including reduction in the risk of certain types of cancer, keeping the skin looking younger and keeping the brain alert.

THE HEDGEROWS WILL be bursting with numerous other fruits in September: among them the blackish-purple elderberry, the deep-purple sloe, the fruit of the blackthorn, used to make sloe gin, and the red berry of the hawthorn. All this fruit provides nourishment for warblers about to head south, and small mammals such as voles, shrews and mice.

THE PATH BENEATH your feet in September will be strewn with hazelnuts, acorns from the oak tree and conkers from the horse chestnut. The acorn is an important source of food for jays, pigeons, ducks, woodpeckers, mice and deer.

I REMEMBER SUSSEX between Pulborough and Storrington one soft still mid-September Thursday: the grapes of the West Chiltington vineyards ripe and ready for picking; the nearby South Downs escarpment shimmering in the late summer haze; the tributary streams of the Arun reduced to a modest trickle; the profusion of nettles poised to do their worst on every last exposed piece of flesh.

THE CONKER, ENCASED in a prickly green shell, is more versatile than one might think. Traditionally they provide the basis of school or pub competition but they are also used as horse medicines, as additives in shampoo and as a starch substitute, and chemicals extracted from conkers can be used to treat scratches and bruises.

THE ARRIVAL OF autumn sees the appearance of a large variety of fungi. Mushrooms and toadstools are in fact just the visible part of fungi, their invisible parts stretching underground for vast distances, obtaining their energy in decaying matter in the soil. Fungi are best observed in woodland or shady field edges.

IF YOU'RE WALKING in deciduous woodland, fungi to look out for at this time of year include the wood blewit, amethyst deceiver with its lilac or purple domed cap, blusher, wood mushroom, porcelain fungus, sulphur tuft, cep, common yellow russula and woolly milk cap.

IN GRASSLAND YOU may find the beautifully named fairy-ring champignon, shaggy ink cap, blackening wax cap and giant puffball. Not all fungi have romantic or quaint names: another that appears in the autumn in coniferous woodland is the sickener which has a seductive bright red cap but, as the name might suggest, is poisonous.

ALFRED WAINWRIGHT ON his 1938 Pennine journey which began in September, and his first encounter with heather: 'A clean wind was blowing... The sight of heather is to me like the sound of a band to marching men – it encourages and stimulates energy.'

I RECALL SEPTEMBER on the West Highland Way in Scotland, and the remarkable changeability of the Scottish weather – rain crashing down so intensely at the hotel in Inverarnan at the head of Loch Lomond that it was impossible to distinguish it from the rush of the nearby waterfall; rain and mist blanketing Rannoch Moor and the Devil's Staircase; then two days later, crystal clear skies, brilliant sunshine and unrivalled clarity for the conquest of Ben Nevis, and the feeling you could forgive nature for every drop of that rain.

Wildlife

THE ABUNDANCE OF acorns and hazelnuts may also provide an abundance of squirrels on the ground as they forage for and then store this food for the winter. The grey squirrel is widespread in southern Britain, while the red is confined to northern Britain and offshore islands in southern Britain, including the Isle of Wight.

THE SIGHT OF salmon leaping, to escape capture or get rid of parasites, is common in Scottish rivers, salmon will often leap substantial waterfalls in the autumn as they seek to get upstream to their spawning grounds. Walkers particularly by the River Tay or Tummel in central Scotland may get a glimpse of this phenomenon.

BIRDWATCHING WALKERS NOTE: September is the start of the great getaway for summer-visiting migrants. These will include swallows, swifts, warblers, flycatchers and chats, as well as butterflies and moths. Their precise time of departure will depend on the weather in September; if the weather is good, you may see them lingering well into the month.

SEPTEMBER SEES THE start of the red deer rut, regarded as one of the greatest spectacles of the autumn calendar, as males confront one another in a bid to become the dominant stag. Rutting can take place at any time of day, though it usually peaks around dawn and dusk.

AT THE SAME time as birds leaving our shores in September, coastal and riverside walkers may notice the arrival from the Arctic of waders around our shorelines and estuaries, in particular the short-legged turnstone, grey-and-white sanderling, knot and purple sandpiper. Huge numbers of knot will congregate on the Wash right through the winter.

NOT ALL THESE birds are here to stay. Poole Harbour is an example of an area of coastline where at this time of year waders will linger only a while before continuing south to southern Europe and Africa, sharing the mudflats with winter residents such as redshank, curlew and dunlin who themselves will have migrated from further north. A true bounty for the coastal walker.

ANOTHER PHENOMENON ASSOCIATED with the arrival of autumn is the flight of baby spiders, or spiderlings; though they can't fly, they will spin a thread known as gossamer to help carry them aloft in order to colonise new areas. As you walk on an autumn morning you may see the ground draped with thousands of these threads.

Where to Walk in September

ALTHOUGH DAYS ARE getting shorter in September, there's still plenty of daylight and early September can often be very warm – but with a heat less ferocious than in August. At the same time, schools are returning so popular holiday destinations won't be so busy. With all that in mind, take on a challenge in September, perhaps one of our longer or tougher national trails.

THE PENNINE WAY runs for some 260 miles, linking the Peak District in Derbyshire with the Cheviots on the border of England and Scotland. Highlights include Kinder Scout, Malham Cove, Pen-y-Ghent, Keld, High Force, High Cup and Hadrian's Wall. It's the oldest national trail and while not as formidable as it once was, there's plenty of tough walking and you'll need about three weeks to complete it.

AS A SLIGHTLY gentler alternative to the Pennine Way, try the Pennine Bridleway. At the time of writing this trail is still incomplete, but what is on offer is a splendid walk of around 130 miles starting from Middleton Top in the White Peak area of Derbyshire and heading through both the White and Dark Peak to Rossendale on the fringes of Manchester. There's some tremendous walking, particularly around Hayfield, just west of Kinder Scout.

THE SOUTHERN UPLAND Way is Scotland's official coast to coast route, running for 212 miles between Portpatrick near Stranraer on the Irish Sea coast, and Cockburnspath near Dunbar on the North Sea coast. In between it traverses some of the most remote terrain in southern Scotland. Highlights include the lovely St Mary's Loch, the Lammermuir Hills and the lofty former mining village of Wanlockhead.

TRY THE 134-MILE Glyndwr's Way, a splendid journey through mid-Wales from Knighton to Welshpool. Again there's a mix of strenuous climbing and more gentle rolling scenery, and although there are some attractive towns and villages en route, including Llanidloes and Machynlleth, a lot of the walking is very remote.

WITH BIRDS BEGINNING their migration from Britain in early autumn, Spurn Head near Hull, a rich mosaic of beach, saltmarsh, mudflats, dunes, grassland and lagoons, is one of the best places to walk and observe the multitude of songbirds as they head to their winter quarters in southern Europe and Africa.

THE NORTH DOWNS Way, a 125-mile national trail from Farnham in Surrey to Dover in Kent, the Garden of England, offers plenteous fruit not only from the hedgerows but from the profusion of apple orchards you'll see on the way – there's also a vineyard right on the route. Scenic highlights include Box Hill, Samphire Hoe and Shakespeare Cliff.

September Wisdom

THE REWARDS OF an early morning walk are plentiful. 'Seven in the morning, dew is on the ground, misty on the grasses bending all round; looking for the berries – what a treasure store! Sweet and black and glossy, who could ask for more? What matter if my trousers are soaked with morning dew? What matter if the socks are likewise soggy too?' (Julia Moore)

A WALK OF several consecutive days will require you to carry day-to-day needs on your back. So practise walking with a full backpack in advance, even if you're only stuffing it with old newspapers. You'll see how it does slow you down but also you can learn to get comfortable in it, adjusting the straps to take your weight most effectively.

MAKE SURE THAT when you've finished packing for real you can bear the load. To lighten and/or spread the rucksack load, use all the pockets available; pack lighter clothes for evening wear; consider whether you can put things in your coat/trouser pockets or even round your neck. And maybe send dirty clothing home as you go (but do warn your long-suffering partner in advance!) and/or arrange to have fresh clothing sent on ahead.

REMEMBER THAT IT'S the sharpest object in your rucksack that will inevitably find its way into a position where it can stab you somewhere in the back, and if there's a single hole in the fabric, any objects small enough to escape through it will invariably find their way to the aforementioned exit! So pack carefully and check the condition of your rucksack regularly but especially prior to a long walking expedition.

YOU WILL ALSO need to take more care when carrying a pack. For instance, if your path divides into parallel sections that are respectively walkable and unwalkable, one higher than the other, it's dangerous to jump from one to another while wearing a heavy pack, the weight of which can cause compression fractures and spinal injury.

MAKE SURE CONTACT details of taxi firms, accommodation that you've booked, and other key contact information gets locked into your mobile phone – saves having to write lists which may get buried in your rucksack when you need them.

WHEN TACKLING A long-distance route, never rely on waymarking alone. Signposts and waymark discs are vulnerable to the weather, to invasive vegetation and, sadly, vandalism and souvenir hunters. Always have a map with you, either traditional paper or on your mobile or tablet, preferably to a 1:25,000 scale. The Ordnance Survey Explorer maps, drawn to this scale, are by far the best.

Notes

1
....

2
....

3
....

4
....

5
....

6
....

7
....

8
....

9
....

10
....

11
....

12
....

13
....

14
....

September

15
....

16
....

17
....

18
....

19
....

20
....

21
....

22
....

23
....

24
....

25
....

26
....

27
....

28
....

29
....

30
....

October

Landscape

OCTOBER 18 IS St Luke's Day, and folklore has it that around this date there is what is called St Luke's Little Summer, a short succession of mild golden autumn days given to us by the saint in question – and indeed in recent years there have been some gloriously warm mid-October days, a true blessing for the autumn walker.

I RECALL THE slopes of Black Down above Haslemere on the Surrey/Sussex border one Friday in early October: the damp grasses dotted with a thousand silk spider webs; some fungi poking tentatively above ground, others forming ledges on the sides of trees; brilliant white woolly mist sitting on the fields and woods below, now and again relenting and parting like opera stage curtains after the overture has ended.

OCTOBER CAN BE a very unsettled and in particular a very windy month. This is because cold polar air is moving south and meeting warm air from the tropics and forming an area of disturbance right over Britain. Southern England's Great Storm, the one famously *not* forecast by Michael Fish, occurred on 16 October 1987.

THESE HIGH WINDS can pose a danger for walkers not only in exposed places but also near trees which, if their root systems are structurally weakened – for instance, by new building developments – may be more likely to fall. So be careful when outdoors in exceptionally windy weather and be prepared to change your plans.

WITH THE RAIN comes mud and standing water so it may be time to discard the trainers which have served you well in summer, and get out the walking boots.

IF YOU'RE WALKING in deciduous woods in October you won't fail to notice the change in colour in deciduous trees such as the oak, ash and beech, a prelude to the shedding of their leaves. This is in fact a survival strategy; with the fall in temperatures, trees can't photosynthesise to produce energy, so it makes sense to shed leaves which would otherwise consume energy.

THERE ARE TWO other practical reasons for the trees to shed leaves; it enables them to preserve their water content, as the total surface area of the tree is reduced, and the strengthening winds will meet less resistance as they blow through bare branches, rendering the trees less likely to be blown over.

October

NOT ONLY DO the leaves of the trees turn golden brown in the autumn: watch also for the changing colour of the bracken, which is widespread on moorland, heathland and common land across Britain but seen to particularly good effect in the North York Moors and Ashdown Forest in East Sussex.

ALFRED WAINWRIGHT DESCRIBED his close encounter with bracken in his Pennine Journey in October 1938: 'The patches of golden bracken were aflame, glistening as if each curling frond held a fairy light.' And about the October sun after the rain: 'The trees still dripped… as I walked beneath them in the bright sunlight I could have filled my hands with falling diamonds.'

October

THE FINAL WEEKEND in October sees the clocks going back an hour, signifying the most obvious transition to winter mode in Britain. While at the start of the month it's still light till 6.30 p.m., by the end it's dark around 4.30 p.m. A lot of lost walking time!

I RECALL THE Yorkshire Wolds Way one crystal clear Friday in late October: watching my feet carefully as I lowered myself down the dewy smooth green of the dry valley hillside; the trees of the plantations of Comber Dale a symphony of red and gold and orange and brown; the triumphal ascent of the valley to another Yorkshire panorama.

OCTOBER IS THE start of the pumpkin season, and if you're walking in the countryside you may see an accumulation of this vegetable, the most famous type of winter squash. It is an excellent source of fibre, rich in antioxidants, is very low in calories and is recommended by dieticians for cholesterol control and weight reduction programmes.

Wildlife

WE SAW HOW the red deer rut began in September, but it is in October that it is most impressive in the Cairngorms, where the glens can resound to the noise of rutting stags; listening to this, under the superb night skies of northern Scotland, will be an unforgettable experience for the night walker.

ANOTHER MAGICAL OCTOBER moment for an observant walker would be to spot the dormouse, which hibernates for a greater period than any other British mammal. At this time of year the dormouse descends to ground level from its hedgerow having feasted on the abundance of September fruits, and weaves a nest among the leaves on the forest floor or beneath a hedgerow. Other creatures, including the hedgehog, will also be preparing to hibernate at this time.

THE SOUNDS OF the forest may not be confined to animals; there is also, in the words of Surrey naturalist Trevor Jones, the 'cascade of the green nut containing husks from the Spanish chestnuts, and the sound of them striking the ground can be quite startling.'

OCTOBER SEES THE arrival of the stunning waxwing, with its fine yellow wings and warm brown plumage, arriving from breeding grounds in Scandinavia and Arctic Russia in search of food. The number of arrivals varies year by year, but in some years huge flocks will turn up on the east coast and head inland, the flocks breaking up only later in winter.

October

OCTOBER ALSO SEES the acceleration of a phenomenon which will have begun in late September, when female grey seals will haul themselves out onto beaches and give birth to a single pup. Their appearance will be confined to colonies where they feel safe including islands off north-west Scotland and Northumberland, and sites off Lincolnshire and north Norfolk.

DURING THIS MONTH hundreds of thousands of wild geese arrive to winter in Britain from their breeding grounds in such places as Canada, Greenland and Siberia, coming in search of food and milder conditions, with particularly large numbers gathering in Islay off western Scotland, the Loch of Strathbeg in eastern Scotland, and north Norfolk.

THE PALE-BELLIED BRENT geese will come from Greenland and eastern Canada and are found around the estuaries of south and east Britain; pink-footed geese come from Iceland and some 100,000 of them gather in north Norfolk over the winter months; and barnacle geese come from Spitsbergen, Svalbard and frequent the north and west coast and marshes.

TWO SPECIES OF swan also arrive from the Arctic in October, namely the whooper swan and Bewick's swan. Both winter in flooded meadows, marshes and lakes. Whooper swans can often be found in very large noisy flocks in V formation, family groups remaining together during migration and over the winter. While the Bewick's swan is the smallest European swan, with black legs and feet, and a black bill with a yellow patch at the base; the shape is unique to every single bird, enabling individual birds to be recognised.

Where to Walk in October

TAKE A WALK in your nearest patch of deciduous or mixed woodland, or, if you live in an urban area, try a walk in your nearest park which contains such woodland. In this way you can enjoy the changing autumn colours, the shades of gold, russet, rich red and brown at their majestic best and, especially on windy days (of which there'll be plenty this month), see the leaves dropping from the trees.

DESPITE TRAFFIC NOISE from Hyde Park Corner in central London, the adjacent Hyde Park offers a range of trees, shrub beds and herbaceous plantings which provide rich habitats for song birds. The Serpentine, Hyde Park's best-known water, attracts a wide range of wildfowl and bats. A great place for the walker to take time out from the busy London streets. In outer London, Hampstead Heath is an important wildlife refuge where you may find grass snakes, foxes, rabbits, slow-worms, squirrels and frogs, while Richmond Park is the top UK site for ancient trees, particularly oaks, and it supports many species of fungi.

IF LONDON LACKS appeal, travel northwards from the capital for an hour, alight at Wendover and wander into the Buckinghamshire beechwoods, following the Ridgeway National Trail westwards to Princes Risborough via Coombe Hill and Cadsden, or eastwards to Tring in Hertfordshire via Haddington Hill, the highest point in Buckinghamshire.

TRAVEL DOWN TO West Sussex and enjoy a walk in Petworth Park with its abundance of fine and ancient deciduous trees, including oak, limes and sweet chestnuts, plus superb views towards the woodlands of Blackdown, the highest ground in Sussex.

GOING FURTHER STILL from London, the Yorkshire Wolds Way National Trail, which runs for 79 miles between Hessle on Humberside and Filey in east Yorkshire, contains many beautiful patches of deciduous woodland, perhaps at its prettiest between Goodmanham and Wharram le Street via Nunburnholme, Millington, Fridaythorpe and Thixendale.

THERE ARE A number of parks where you may observe both fallow and red deer taking part in the annual rut. As well as Richmond Park two other parks to observe the deer rut are Petworth, as mentioned above, and Fountains Abbey in North Yorkshire.

THE NATIONAL TRUST organise a number of Halloween walks, for those seeking to 'celebrate' the annual festival of all things ghostly and ghoulish. Google 'National Trust Halloween' for events taking place in your region.

October Wisdom

WITH SO MUCH wet, windy weather this month, you may find yourself shopping for foul weather gear. Choose a brightly coloured garment as this will not only be more cheerful to wear in the rain but will also enable you to be seen more clearly in the event of an accident. Another good investment is a weatherproof map cover – much cheaper than buying 'all-weather' maps.

WHILE WALKING IN woodland it can be frighteningly easy to lose your sense of direction, and one path can look just like any other. Don't assume that a gap between the trees must be 'the path' and don't be seduced by forest tracks which look as though they must be 'the path' but in reality may well not be, and may take you very far from the correct route. Do keep alert and watch for helpful landmarks, whether manmade or natural – they could be as basic as a pile of logs or a grotesquely shaped tree.

THE GROUND IS littered at this time of year with chestnut burrs and fallen leaves, and after a woodland walk you may come back with burrs from various plants stuck to your clothing including your socks and your footwear. The Internet is full of ideas for removing them, such as the use of duct tape, a butter knife, comb or air compressor with nozzle. Or you may find a certain therapeutic value in just pulling at the wretched things.

LOWLAND WALKING OFTEN brings with it more fiddly route-finding. If you're following a route using a map, and what you see isn't what you expect, you can 99 times out of 100 be sure that it's not the map that's at fault. Check first and foremost, by the surrounding landmarks, that you've not inadvertently strayed from the route, e.g. following an indentation in a field left by a tractor rather than the correct footpath.

AN EQUALLY LIKELY explanation for divergence between the map and the reality is that the landowner has altered the land by, say, cutting down areas of woodland or removing field boundary fences and hedges. This may result in path diversions or even closures. Where there's an obvious conflict between map and path signage, follow the route indicated by the signage.

IF YOU SET out in dry weather but wet weather is forecast, make sure, if you're not wearing your wet weather gear, it's at the top of your pack so that if it starts raining suddenly you are able to get at it straight away. Also ensure that if you finish your walk in dry weather and cagoule-free that you remember to extract your cagoule from your rucksack and air it.

FOOTPATH SIGNAGE IN woodland other than access land is usually excellent and the absence of any signage at clear junctions of woodland tracks is a fair indication that you've gone wrong. Be prepared to backtrack to the last signed junction. And don't risk short cuts which may get you into worse trouble. If you're walking in large areas of woodland access land without path signage, a compass or GPS technology is a must.

Notes

1

2

3

4

5

6

7

8

9

10

11

12

13

14

October

15
....

16
....

17
....

18
....

19
....

20
....

21
....

22
....

23
....

24
....

25
....

26
....

27
....

28
....

29
....

30
....

31
....

November

Landscape

I RECALL NOVEMBER on Beacon Hill above South Harting on the South Downs: an almost vertical ascent on a path made slippery by the rain and mud; the joy of gaining the top and striding across the springy grass and, as the rain cleared, gazing out across the Downs under lightening skies to the sea and the Isle of Wight beyond, a real autumn gift from nature.

I HAVE CLEAR, though not hugely fond, recollections of Crowborough Beacon in East Sussex one Saturday afternoon in early November where an obstinate fog hung on the highest slopes: tiny fountains thrown up by the crunch of the boot on the saturated heather; a flat, ghostly, windless calm; tracks leading only to destination grey white; heather and trees alike seemingly drained of colour.

COLOUR IS AT a premium with the majority of wild plants having lost their flowers by the time November arrives. But there are some splashes of colour, including the blue flowers of the common field speedwell, the white flowers of the yarrow in grassland and the lilac of the ivy-leaved toadflax on walls and rocks.

THERE ARE A number of other plants which an observant walker may see that are still in flower. Among them are the rounded oval flower-heads of the pineapple mayweed, widespread on tracks, and the small yellow flower-heads of the common ragwort, found in grassland, grazed verges and waste ground.

EVEN ALLOWING FOR the lessening hours of daylight, sunshine in November is well down on that in October: 43 fewer sunshine hours in Sussex and 37 hours less in Yorkshire. Kinlochewe in western Scotland enjoys just 23 hours of sunshine in November.

I VIVIDLY REMEMBER the beechwoods of Buckinghamshire one golden mid-November Saturday afternoon: some browning leaves clinging to the trees as if in denial of their imminent fate; each footstep throwing up a confetti of the shrivelled specimens that had taken the plunge; a weak watery mid-afternoon sun poking through bare branches; the pace quickening at the prospect of hot scones and honey in the Willow Tree tea room at Amersham.

SNOW IS UNUSUAL in November but not unknown. As recently as 2010 there were significant falls of snow right across Britain and in parts of Scotland. On 28 November 2010 there was the phenomenon of thundersnow – heavy snow accompanied by thunder and lightning – double trouble for would-be walkers.

NOVEMBER DOES BRING plenty of rain. It was as recently as November 2009 that Seathwaite in Cumbria, which has one of the highest average rainfall totals in Britain, saw an astonishing (and record) 495 mm of rain in just four days. The highest day's rainfall ever recorded in Wales, 211 mm, was in November 1929 in Mid Glamorgan.

IT JUST GOES on getting darker; by the end of November the sun will be setting at just gone 4 p.m. in the south of England and just gone 3.30 p.m. in the north of Scotland, with barely 7 hours of daylight overall.

BUT AN INDIAN summer can spring delightful surprises for the November walker. Trevor Jones writing on 20 November 1978, after one of the hottest autumns on record: 'One is still and constantly delighted by the vivid colours of trees and hedges, the long lingering of flowers and the amazingly lush greens of pastures, winter wheat and lawns.'

THERE MAY STILL be plenty of fungi to be found. One species, the yellow stagshorn fungus, doesn't appear until late autumn. It's widespread and fairly common in coniferous woodland and is readily recognised by its yellow antler-like growths.

NOVEMBER BRINGS ITS own special fragrances, perhaps best experienced by a village walker on a crisp cold early evening close to Guy Fawkes Night: the fragrance of wood burning stoves; the smoke of autumn bonfires; and the mischievous hint of sulphur left by fireworks, themselves bringing flashes of colour to the dark night sky.

ONE OF THE most obvious indicators to the November walker of the onset of autumn is the turning of the leaves of the silver birch tree. With its thin silvery-grey bark and triangular leaves the silver birch is one of the most easily recognised trees, its small cones releasing tiny papery-winged seeds. It is widespread across Britain, including in upland areas; in exposed or cold locations the leaves can be expected to have turned and fallen by November but silver birches in sheltered spots may retain their green leaves right through the month.

I RECALL MID-NOVEMBER along a Sussex lane beside Hammerponds, huge artificial ponds at watermills: after days and weeks of rain, the landscape bathed in balmy sunshine, some trees now stripped of their summer clothing, some stubbornly retaining it and others now attired in glorious autumn gold.

Wildlife

As you enjoy the November night, don't just smell but listen. This time of year may see invasions of short-eared owls from Continental Europe, having found there is a shortage of food in their traditional breeding areas because of bad weather or reduced populations of the voles on which they feed.

Despite the migration of summer visitors, there are still many resident birds and winter visitors for the birdwatching walker to enjoy, beside the geese and swans. They include redwings, fieldfares, chaffinches, blackbirds, house and hedge sparrows, the three tit species and nuthatch.

It's a great time for walkers to observe starlings. Our starling population will be joined by millions of starlings from the Arctic, and as dusk falls they will join together in flocks, perhaps the most impressive being among the reedbeds on the Somerset Levels.

The pied wagtail, a songbird with black and white plumage, is another bird that gathers in large flocks at dusk on a November evening in search of light and heat. They may be found in very urban locations such as on industrial estates or in ornamental trees in shopping centres – something to look out for when city or town walking this month.

By the time the shops have shut and shoppers are wending their way home there may be as many as a thousand wagtails gathered together in a single roost, thriving on the warmth generated by the mass of human bodies below them!

Observant walkers in the remote glens and forests of the Highlands of Scotland in November may be rewarded with the sight of a young wildcat. A wildcat will have produced a single litter of up to seven kittens in the spring, and by November these kittens will have matured and be setting out for the first time.

During this time of year the kittens will take advantage of the first snowfalls, seeking to creep up on potential prey such as rabbits, hares, voles and mice as these creatures themselves seek food; they will also feed on the dead bodies of animals unable to survive the cold.

Bats will be winding down towards their winter sleep, having fed hard in summer and early autumn to build up their fat reserves. Observant and fortunate walkers may see that they have now become increasingly cold and sluggish and will enter trees, caves and even disused buildings to hibernate.

Where to Walk in November

ALTHOUGH SNOW IN November is rare, it can often be wet and gloomy, not the best weather for hill walking and enjoying the views. If it's bucketing with rain or blowing a gale and you don't fancy venturing out into the countryside, but you've still got itchy feet, consider a city walk. Wherever you are in mainland Britain, save in the very far north, you're within reach of a rewarding one.

THE ULTIMATE CITY walks are to be found in the capital cities of London and Edinburgh. One day will suffice to enjoy a walking tour of London's principal attractions including St Paul's Cathedral, Trafalgar Square, Westminster Abbey, the Houses of Parliament and Big Ben, while the Royal Mile and Princes Street, the most famous streets in Edinburgh, are only a few minutes apart; you could spend a whole day on the Royal Mile alone.

THE CITY OF York contains a fabulous array of year-round attractions including its breathtaking minster, National Railway Museum, Jorvik Viking Museum and Castle Museum with its replica Victorian street. Then after dark join a ghost walk through York's famous snickelways and prepare to be convinced – and afraid.

THE CITY OF Bath is a Georgian treasure house. A short circular tour will incorporate the glorious Pulteney Bridge over the wide fast-flowing waters of the Avon, the Pump Room and site of the Roman baths, the nearby abbey and the opulent Royal Crescent, some of the finest Regency architecture in Britain.

COMPARE THE CLASSIC university cities of Oxford and Cambridge, Oxford with its Bodleian Library, Radcliffe Camera and Christ Church Meadows. Cambridge with the imposing King's College, St John's College, Bridge of Sighs and the Backs, and if the sun shines, a charming autumn riverside walk to Grantchester, immortalised by the war poet Rupert Brooke.

A SMALLER CITY, but city nonetheless and with huge charm and beauty, is Chichester in West Sussex. Dominated by its magnificent eleventh-century cathedral, its four main streets, converging on the sixteenth-century cross, and the side streets behind, are packed with fine Georgian architecture, best observed from the superbly preserved ancient city walls. The cathedral tower in recent years has been host to peregrine falcons and indeed these birds can nest on tall buildings in many urban areas.

IF YOU WANT a great wildlife experience in November, visit Donna Nook just south-east of Cleethorpes in Lincolnshire. In this area of saltmarsh, as in a number of other parts of Britain, the grey seal population returns to breed between October and December and gives birth to pups on the sandbanks. If you've never seen a seal in the wild before, look no further.

November Wisdom

THOUGH IT MAY seem incongruous, wearing shorts during a downpour isn't a bad idea, even in November, providing temperatures are mild. A pair of polyester sports shorts take up negligible rucksack space, will dry very easily and quickly and won't trap your body in cold clammy fabric which continues to cause discomfort long after the rain has stopped. Bear in mind that some sports shorts aren't equipped with pockets so you'll need to set aside some dry rucksack space for your valuables.

IN VERY WET or muddy conditions, you may care to complement your shorts with gaiters (effectively an extra layer of fabric secured round your lower leg and ankle) which protect your socks and upper boot areas from the worst effects of rain or mud and aren't as cumbersome as overtrousers. The time taken putting them on is time well spent.

UNLESS YOU'RE IN serious walking country, don't assume that the owner of the pub or cafe you stop at will welcome you into his/her establishment with your muddy boots and dripping gaiters. In the absence of any indication to the contrary, remove them at the front door.

AS WINTER DRAWS nearer and the nights draw in, there is perhaps greater potential for things to go wrong. If walking in remote rugged terrain, it's prudent to carry a whistle round your neck on a lanyard so you can summon help in an emergency – remember you may not get a signal on your phone. The recognised distress signal is six blasts on the whistle repeated at one-minute intervals.

EVEN IF YOU'RE walking only by day and along roads or lanes, consider investing in a high-visibility jacket or gilet. True, it may make you look like a council workman, but in the murky conditions that November often brings, it will enable you to be seen not only by your fellow walkers but by other road users. When mist is about and/or darkness is falling, a torch is also essential, both to see and be seen.

WHEN ROAD WALKING and there's no pavement, the conventional wisdom is to walk on the right-hand side, i.e. the same side as oncoming traffic, but it may be safest to cross over when the road bends to the right or the grass verge is wider on the other side.

REMEMBER THAT WHILE road walking is faster and less fiddly than path walking, footpaths often – for historical reasons – provide a much more direct route from village to village. Double check your map for footpath links on your chosen route.

Notes

1 ....

2 ....

3 ....

4 ....

5 ....

6 ....

7 ....

8 ....

9 ....

10 ....

11 ....

12 ....

13 ....

14 ....

November

15

16

17

18

19

20

21

22

23

24

25

26

27

28

29

30

December

Landscape

MAYBE BECAUSE THEY'RE 'dreaming of a white Christmas' many believe December brings with it the coldest weather of the year. In many parts of Britain the average maximum and minimum temperature for December is actually higher than it is in January – albeit in north-west Scotland there is no difference, the average minimum in Kinlochewe being a chilly 0.9 degrees Celsius throughout December, January and February; in December Kinlochewe endures an average 12 days of air frost.

I REMEMBER THE walk to Middleton from Tamworth in Warwickshire one Saturday morning in mid-December: the slap of the bitter cold on my face on leaving the warmth of the train; a dusting of fresh snow on the fields out-whiting even the bright white of Middleton's timber-framed cottages; the footpath to the Old Smithy, a Christmas card scene made real; the churchyard nestling among sunlit conifers.

ANYWHERE IN BRITAIN, however, there's the danger of another seasonal phenomenon, freezing rain. When it falls, it's potentially fatal to unwary walkers – inoffensive enough in the air, but creating a lethal layer of ice as soon as it hits the ground, turning every road and pavement into a skating rink.

As FOR RAIN, on average Sheffield sees more rain in December (86.7 mm) than in any other month of the year, and in western Scotland only January is wetter, December seeing 263 mm of the stuff with just 14.6 hours of sunshine, far lower than any other month of the year. By contrast, Bognor Regis on the Sussex coast enjoys an average of 66.7 hours of December sunshine.

THE AMOUNT OF sunshine is of course partially dictated by the amount of daylight. The shortest day is officially the 21 December, with less than 8 hours between sunrise and sunset in London, but as around the longest day, the differences in lengths of days for the two weeks either side of the shortest day are negligible.

IN LONDON, FOR instance, in the month between 21 December and 21 January just 7 minutes of extra daylight will be gained in the morning, the sun actually rising a few minutes *later* for a few days after 21 December!

I RECALL THE walk from Lulworth to Weymouth on the Dorset coast on another mid-December Saturday morning: Lulworth stripped of the crowds and souvenirs and ice cream; mild air rushing at me on a south-westerly wind, trying to push me back as I struggled up and down the relentless succession of climbs and drops on the utterly exposed hillside above Durdle Door; somewhere on the horizon, when I could dare to look, a place where the swirling grey of the sea met the angry grey of the sky.

BY THIS TIME of year, most deciduous trees will be bare, although especially if the autumn has been mild, some greeny-brown leaves will still cling on well into the month. However, green foliage will remain on evergreens such as the holly, box and rhododendron, providing continuing woodland colour for December walkers.

MOST EVERGREENS ARE conifers, among them native species such as Scots pine, juniper and yew and non-native species such as the Douglas fir and Norway spruce, better known as the Christmas tree! Douglas firs grow to a tremendous height, and indeed the tallest tree in England (to be found near Dunster in Somerset) is a Douglas fir; at 60 metres high, it's taller than Nelson's Column.

December

WE ALL KNOW the carol 'The Holly and the Ivy'; it's a reminder that these two plants bear fruit in December, as well as another plant linked inexorably with the festive season, mistletoe. The ivy is a climbing plant which you will often find on house walls; a nuisance to homeowners but delightful for town and village walkers! Ivy produces small black berries which are an important food source for songbirds that spend the winter here, particularly thrushes.

MISTLETOE, IN COMMON with holly and ivy, was regarded by ancient druids as a safeguard against evil. It can be seen growing high in the branches of trees including oak and apple and being an evergreen, becomes much more noticeable when its host's leaves have been shed. At this time of year it produces clumps of berries which are white and sticky.

I HAVE HUGELY fond recollections of a York city walk one late Saturday afternoon just before Christmas: the bright lights of the city streets seemingly squeezing the last fragments of grey light from the day; shop window displays along Stonegate competing for seasonal quaintness; the sounds of carolling buskers at Goodramgate; a hungry queue stretching back from the entrance to Betty's tea rooms; windswept worshippers hurrying to the minster for choral evensong.

Wildlife

THE BIRD THAT is most synonymous with December and the Christmas season in particular is the robin. Robins are regular visitors to neighbourhoods when temperatures drop, as they come in search of food, so don't be surprised to see them on a brisk post-Christmas stroll. The association with Christmas dates back to early postmen being nicknamed 'robins' because they wore red uniforms, and Victorian artists then put robins on the cards they were delivering!

EVEN IF YOU don't see robins, you may hear them. Although other songbirds flock together in the winter months, robins defend their territory throughout the winter, so need to sing as much in December as in any other month of the year.

AS YOU WALK among coniferous woodland in December, watch for the crossbill, a bird which exists solely on conifer seeds; it may be seen taking seeds from the cones to feed both itself and its young, and indeed it is perfectly possible for crossbill eggs to be laid at this time of year.

WHILE ON THE edge of the woods, look out for the brambling, a bird that's a winter visitor to Britain; the male is readily recognised by its salmon pink breast and white rump, and yellow bill with black tip, while the female boasts pale buff underparts.

AS YOU ENJOY a bracing coastal walk in December, look out for the kingfisher. Though these beautiful birds of orange and blue usually frequent freshwater rivers and wetlands, they may sometimes prefer coastal estuaries and harbours in colder weather.

THOUGH ONE MIGHT associate moths with the balmy days of summer, a number of moths are still active in December; these are species which don't appear as adults until the autumn. They have rather drab grey-brown colouring but very delicate markings and though nocturnal can sometimes be seen at dusk.

Where to Walk in December

IF YOU'VE HAD a fall of fresh snow, head for the nearest pine woodland and enjoy the contrast of white and green and the crunch of your feet in the newly accumulated flakes.

IF YOU'RE SUFFICIENTLY well-equipped, and can find a torch that works, choose a clear starry night and enjoy a night walk. Take a telescope and choose a lofty summit or other location which offers the best range of stars. Why not see the New Year in on a hilltop and gaze down at the firework displays below? The champagne can keep till the morning!

YOU MAY NOT feel up to tackling one of the established national trails or other 'named' paths this month, given short days and pre-Christmas activities, so with pubs offering tempting Christmas fare during December, why not create your own pub walk or series of pub walks, linking the best real ale pubs? Even if it takes time to perfect the optimum routes, you'll enjoy doing the research!

SHOPPING IN LARGE towns or cities in the run-up to Christmas is no fun. And nor is trudging through mud or flooded fields, legacies of the autumn rains. So spend a December day exploring an attractive small town near you on foot, this time looking out for all the features of interest in both its main thoroughfares and quieter streets.

December

TRY A WALK in one of these gems: Stamford in Lincolnshire, Battle in East Sussex, Chipping Campden in Gloucestershire, Holt in Norfolk, Hexham in Northumberland, Great Torrington in Devon or Richmond in North Yorkshire. Not only will you enjoy exploring the historical and scenic aspects of these towns but you can shop for Christmas gifts that may be unavailable in larger chains – and help the local economy at the same time.

IF NONETHELESS YOU want a December challenge, try the 45 miles of the Norfolk Coast Path (the other half of the Peddars Way) between Hunstanton and Cromer – easy to access, less vulnerable than the hills and mountains to the excesses of winter, and host to a massive variety of wintering birds, as described above.

OR ENJOY A walk on your favourite sandy beach. Beaches aren't just for lounging on in the heat of summer – they offer huge rewards for the winter walker. Go when the tide is right out – tide tables for the sea area concerned are posted on the Internet – and appreciate the full range of shorescapes, not just the water, sand, shingle and dunes but the sky as well. Among the shingle, look for shells – you'll be amazed and delighted at their variety and intricacy.

A WALK IN the forests south of Dunster in the Exmoor National Park will bring you to some of the tallest conifers in the country.

December Wisdom

BEARING IN MIND the short days of this month, plan to walk a little less than you think you can manage in a day, and be prepared to abandon your walk if conditions become very bad. There is nothing courageous or heroic in pressing on and getting benighted, soaked or frozen. You've the whole of next year to do it all over again.

IF YOU'RE STUCK for items for your Christmas list, what about asking for an annual subscription to one of the many excellent walking magazines? These are superbly illustrated and provide huge numbers of suggestions for walks and expert advice for walkers.

YOUR SUGGESTION OF a bracing Boxing Day family walk may not go down well with your teenage children or grandchildren. But before chiding them too severely for their lack of enthusiasm remember that you were just the same at their age, and tailor the walk accordingly, perhaps ensuring the inclusion of an interesting feature or two en route.

WHY NOT USE some of the lazy post-Christmas days to write up the best local walks you've done this year for your local newspaper. Local papers love this sort of thing – it's refreshing and interesting for readers. You may not get paid for your work, but you'll enjoy writing the pieces and they'll be good on your CV should you seek to get your written work published commercially.

AFTER A WALK in freezing or exceptionally wet conditions, with Christmas goodies awaiting, you may feel especially relieved to get home. But remember, when you get back, don't flop straight down in front of the festive TV but deal with your filthy boots first – or you'll regret it when putting them back on next time. That is if they're in a state to be put back on at all. Hose them down, wipe the mud off and apply dubbin or equivalent. Then have a bath, change and relax!

IF YOU DECIDE to do a night walk, recce it first by day to ensure you won't get lost when you come to do it for real. Darkness can be very disorientating and even with a torch you can't rely on seeing all the landmarks you need.

THE BEST TIP comes last. Turn off the TV, pour yourself a cuppa or a glass of wine and treat yourself to a nostalgic reliving of your walking exploits of the past year. Upload your camera pictures onto your computer. Print the best ones and create a collage for your kitchen noticeboard – a reminder, during the long January days ahead, of great walks, great weather and happy times.

$Notes$

1 ....

2 ....

3 ....

4 ....

5 ....

6 ....

7 ....

8 ....

9 ....

10 ....

11 ....

12 ....

13 ....

14 ....

December

15
....

16
....

17
....

18
....

19
....

20
....

21
....

22
....

23
....

24
....

25
....

26
....

27
....

28
....

29
....

30
....

31
....

Index

Index

Index

Index

Index

Index

Index

The
Seaside
Year

Isobel Carlson

THE SEASIDE YEAR

Isobel Carlson

ISBN: 978 1 84953 697 4

Hardback

£9.99

This charming and practical handbook is bursting with tips, facts and folklore to guide you through a year by the sea. Find out how to identify shells by shape and markings, choose the best coastal routes to explore and learn about the geography of the beautiful beaches and craggy cliffs that Great Britain has to offer.

With handy diary pages for making your own notes each month, this is a must-have for any eager seaside explorer.

If you're interested in finding out more about
our books, find us on Facebook at
Summersdale Publishers
and follow us on Twitter at
@Summersdale.

www.summersdale.com